OUTRUNNING
Age

a memoir

OUTRUNNING

Age

Meeting Midlife
with Courage, Compassion,
and a Few Blisters

MELINDA WALSH

Outrunning Age: Meeting Midlife with Courage, Compassion, and a Few Blisters

Copyright © 2023 by Melinda Walsh

All rights reserved.
No part of this publication may be reproduced, distributed, or transmitted in any form or by any means, including photocopying, recording, or other electronic or mechanical methods, without the prior written permission of the author, except in the case of brief quotations embodied in critical reviews and certain other noncommercial uses permitted by copyright law.

Some names and identifying details have been changed to protect the privacy of individuals.

Published by Creative Spirit Press

To contact the author about booking talks or workshops or ordering books in bulk, visit www.melindawalsh.com.

ISBN (paperback): 978-0-9658293-0-4
ISBN (ebook): 978-0-9658293-1-1

Book coach: Martha Bullen, Bullen Publishing Services
Editor: Jessica Vineyard, Red Letter Editing, LLC, www.redletterediting.com
Book cover design: Jelena Mirkovic
Book interior design: Maggie McLaughlin
Author photos: Thomas Naylor, Jency Hogan

Printed in the United States of America

To my husband, Tom.
In the marathon of life, you are my aid station.

Contents

Preface	Out of One Life and Into Another	ix
Chapter 1	The Starting Line	1
Chapter 2	Getting Back on My Feet	9
Chapter 3	Running The Beast	15
Chapter 4	The Flood	29
Chapter 5	Mud and Mudders	39
Chapter 6	Flying Melinda Wallenda	45
Chapter 7	On the Run Again	53
Chapter 8	Putting My Best Face Forward	61
Chapter 9	The Year of Being Noncommittal	77
Chapter 10	Race Day, Take Two	97
Chapter 11	What's Next?	107
So You Want to Start Exercising		127
Questions for Reflection		131

Preface

Out of One Life and Into Another

*It's impossible, said Pride. It's risky, said Experience.
It's pointless, said Reason.
Give it a try, whispered the Heart.*
—UNKNOWN

I didn't realize it at the time, but I started running out of my first marriage the day I took my stepdaughter's tennis shoes and headed out to the sugarcane fields that surrounded our antebellum home. The day before, I had walked the fifty yards from the front porch, past the three-hundred-year-old oaks, to the mailbox, and was shocked to discover that the walk had made me winded. I put two fingers to my neck and felt my pulse flutter like oak leaves in a Louisiana thunderstorm. As I strolled back, bills in hand, heart racing, I thought, "I am too damn young to be this out of shape." With that declaration, at age thirty-seven, I became a runner before I even took my first step.

It took me a while to own it, however. I thought

runners ran marathons in record time without stopping to catch their breath and collected medals as proof of their efforts. I was too slow to be a real runner, I told myself, so at first I mostly walked through the fields at dusk, the sun raking low over the green tops of the sugar cane. I liked leaving my sneaker tracks alongside those of the raccoons and deer who sometimes shared the headrows with me.

The headrows are the streets of the fields. As I ran, I focused on avoiding tripping over the tractor ruts, a practice that kept me from ruminating too much on the strained state of my once-happy relationship. I also wanted to avoid the heavy feeling in the pit of my stomach whenever I thought back to The Way Things Used To Be and compared them to How They Are Now. I tried to outrun the tears. Sometimes the dog trotted alongside me. I spoke my fears and concerns to her, but she didn't have many answers.

Off I went, ten minutes out, ten minutes back, six days a week, leaping over the occasional snake and getting cut by the stray sugar cane leaf. After two weeks I decided that I either needed go farther or faster, and I chose faster. I could soon run one mile without stopping, then two. Only after six months of this did I commit enough to purchase my own running shoes. I gratefully returned my stepdaughter's shoes to her closet, the mileage on them a little higher.

A year after I first took those shoes, the day came for me to run out of my marriage for real. I packed up my running shoes and wedding silver and ran into my

Out of One Life and Into Another

new life. I was sad and relieved, all at the same time. Running gave me a comforting structure to my days. I missed the headrows, the white-tailed deer, the cycles of the cane, and the raccoon tracks, but I did not miss my fractured marriage as I settled into my new home near several peaceful lakes.

The lakes are populated with herons, visiting white pelicans, and—this being Louisiana—the occasional alligator. Two-story Louisiana State University (LSU) sorority houses line one side of the lake, their plantation-style structure making rippling reflections on the water. Turtles catch the sun on partially submerged logs, lining up like railroad cars, the biggest one in the prime spot and the rest arranged in hierarchical rows. Cypress, live oak, and mimosa trees—Louisiana ambassadors—stand proudly around the perimeter, and the squirrels scold (or maybe encourage) runners as they pass.

'Real runners run here, all the way around the lakes, four miles without stopping', I thought to myself. I wasn't a "real runner" yet, so I just ran two miles in my neighborhood each day, filling the steps with affirmations. I mentally chanted mantras in sync with my pace. *I love myself. I love my body. My body runs easily. My body loves to run.*

However, I also thought, *I am too curvy to be a real runner*. I waited in vain for the miles to make me a broad-shouldered, straight-hipped, no-body-fat runner. My unhelpful comparison to more experienced runners made me blind to the fact that being curvy and busty wouldn't keep me from gradually improving my pace.

Outrunning Age

My leg muscles were strong, and when I tightened them, I was surprised to see that my quadriceps muscles were becoming more defined, and I could now see my leg biceps in the back. I continued to run toward new possibilities with each step.

Having no husband around to occupy my days opened up opportunities to make male friends. One of my first new friends was a long-time runner, as in, I-just-added-up-my-lifetime-mileage-and-it's-enough-to-have-run-around-the-Earth kind of long-time runner. He introduced me to a group of his friends whose idea of travel was to research a city they had never been to and where a marathon was going to be held, and then meet there and run the race. I was in awe of and intimidated by these folks, and I dreamed of one day being able to keep pace with them instead of watching their backs pull away from me.

Hanging out with a pack of elite and seasoned runners was both a good thing and a bad thing. I kept up with my running so that I could be one of them, but I beat myself up because I fell short of their pace. My best-ever time at this point was "only" an eight-minute mile, whereas most of the others ran 7:30s or faster. I mostly hung back in a 9:30 to 10:30 range, not seeing that I was the only one who was judging me. No matter how many miles I ran, I was unable to outrun my self-criticism.

One day a neighbor saw me go out the door in my running clothes and asked, "You running the lakes today?" I launched into my rationale for how I wasn't

Out of One Life and Into Another

a real runner; I didn't run races, and I could only run two miles. The more I talked, though, the more I realized how silly I sounded. In case I missed it, my neighbor burst out laughing and said, "I see you run every day. How can you not call yourself a runner?"

Sometimes it feels good—and terrifying—to face our self-imposed limitations. I immediately took off for a run around the larger of the two LSU lakes—all four miles of it. My ego came along with me and offered such helpful comments as, *You know you can't do this. You can only run a couple of miles. You're really slow, anyway. A ten-minute mile isn't that fast.* Like a lousy friend with a loudspeaker, my ego threw doubts at me with every step, trying to trip up my confidence. Sure enough, I ran out of gas around the two-mile mark, clear on the other side of the lake from my car. I walked for a bit and then ran the rest.

As I unlocked my car and plopped, hot and sweaty, into the driver's seat, it hit me. I had just run the LSU lakes. Damn. Maybe I *was* a runner.

Chapter 1

The Starting Line

Aging is not lost youth but a new stage of opportunity and strength.
—BETTY FRIEDAN

*Age is no barrier.
It's a limitation you put on your mind.*
—JACKIE JOYNER KERSEE

I could tell the second I lowered into the one-legged squat that I was trying one rep too many. My brain told my muscles to fire, and time slowed down.

"Come on, you can do it," my trainer said. I wanted to please this thirty-five-year-old father of two, who wore his hair in a man bun and whose family tattoo was molded over his cut bicep. I had just started working out with a new trainer after a year-long hiatus. Before I had taken the time off from training, I had gone through an intense two-week period during which I got married at age fifty-five, lost my dad, and parted ways with my biggest client. Healing from the psychological changes had taken longer than I had expected, and I was eager to resume regular physical activity.

There was no *pop*, no sudden movement of the dynamic mechanism that was my knee, to herald the injury that happened just then. Instead, the rubber band ligaments that cradled the joint simply stretched past their ability to rebound. I wondered if, at age fifty-seven, I had lost my stretch, as well. I felt like I had just slammed headlong into what it meant to be getting older.

I held on to my trainer's hands, both for dear life and for my future, and gritted my teeth as my body gave its last drop of glucose to help me rise to a wobbly standing position. "Good job!" Man Bun exclaimed, going for the high five. I tried to feel proud of myself, not knowing that one squat too many was going to halt my running and workouts for the next eight months.

The Knee

The day after one-too-many squats, my knee swelled up like a balloon with too much air. Bending it felt weird, but I thought I just needed to lay off it for a week or so. Gradually the swelling came down, and my trainer and I tried new activities. Rowing machine: knee swelled. Cycle warmups: knee swelled. Running: *ouch*. Everything we tried aggravated the pain. The chorus of I-told-you-so's began to swell, too. It seemed like everyone who didn't run had an opinion on running and getting older.

The Starting Line

This is what happens when we age, Melinda. You'll have to learn to slow down. I'll bet with all that running you've done, you have arthritis. My friend Charles had to have a knee replacement last year, and he was only forty-five. With all that running you've done, you've probably torn the meniscus. You'll need surgery. (Thank you for that last diagnosis, my schoolteacher friend.)

What I needed surgery on was my fears. What if they were right? Perhaps I had reached my physical limit, had run my last mile. Maybe this was just me getting old and decrepit.

I suffered for months, even as I visualized health, headed out for a run-walk, and limped back home. *Do I give up?* I wondered if I had waited long enough for it to heal, or if I should give it more time. On top of that, the more my knee hurt, the more wrinkles I saw in my face. Who knew those body parts were connected?

I Want to Be That Person

When my nephew, Brandon, ran the Louisiana Marathon for the first time in 2015, I decided to meet him at the finish line. He had consistently trained as a runner for a couple of years, gradually working up from 5K to 10K races, then to a half-marathon, and finally, a full marathon of 26.2 miles. I wanted to support him and celebrate his having reached such a big milestone.

As I parked, I was surprised at how big the crowd was. My knee was still in pain, but I ran the couple of blocks from my parking spot to where the race ended, making

3

Outrunning Age

my way in a limping run-walk, envious of the runners with racing bibs that proclaimed them as participants.

The finish line for this race was a big deal, with loud music, a giant inflated finish-line structure, and a grandstand. Flags lined the street and whipped in the wind as if applauding the runners as they passed. A big digital clock with each runner's race time counted the minutes and seconds, and I knew that the first marathon runners would be coming in soon. The street was blocked off with guardrails to give the runners plenty of space to keep going past the grandstand and get out of the way of other participants as they crossed the line. The emcee kept the crowd going as the first runners came in, and I was surprised to hear that he announced each runner's name and age as they crossed the line.

The half-marathoners were trickling in as well, and two runners caught my attention: a husband and wife, both in their mid-sixties, smiling and holding hands as they finished together. My knee ached, and my heart did a little, too. I couldn't imagine running 13.1 miles, not with this knee situation. I wondered how they did it, if it was even possible for me, and if I wanted to spend the time, effort, and miles to condition myself.

As I walked with my nephew toward the physical therapy tent to get his legs stretched out, I felt like an outsider amid all the tired athletes. I didn't like the feeling, and I was discouraged that I couldn't see any way of joining this group with my knee injury. Would I ever be able to? I comforted myself with a silly thought: *Maybe I just have a case of the "kneesles," and this too shall pass.*

The Starting Line

Later, as I limped back to my car, I couldn't get the thought of the sixty-year-old woman runner out of my mind. I observed, in myself and others, that letting our world shrink as we collect years was all too easy, that we gradually stop doing the things we could always do before. I knew that living out the story I had about myself—that I was too old or tired or whatever to "do that"—would lead me to choices that made sure "that" would never happen. On the other hand, telling myself that I was able to run a half-marathon brought up doubts. Was I lying to myself? Living in a fantasy?

Our culture is infused with messages that tell us to take care of ourselves as we age by doing less. One of the most challenging visualizations for me was to imagine myself doing something that didn't seem possible, to ignore current circumstances and "proof" that I couldn't do them. However, a directive deep inside me drove me to challenge my limitations, to find out whether they were self-imposed or physically grounded. I knew that my aging body would gradually eliminate some options all by itself, but I didn't have to help it along.

It was time to face the fact that my knee wasn't going to heal on its own. I had to find out if I needed surgery.

The Ortho and the MRI

I braced myself for the visit to the orthopedist, who would ostensibly render judgment on what was wrong with my knee. He was a kind man whose own torn meniscus had ended his running career. I kept that in mind as he gently manipulated my swollen knee. I wondered if his personal history meant he would lean toward surgery for me. I was watchful.

"We have a choice," he said. "We can just watch it a bit more or get an MRI and see what's going on. That can tell us what to do next." This made sense to me, so two days later I was meditating in the MRI room while the magic of a powerful magnetic field and an electric current pulsing through my body opened a window into the structure of my knee. I could sense that I was at a psychic intersection, with one path leading to surgery and the curtailing of my activities, and the other, a miracle that nothing was actually wrong. I could feel the expectations of the medical community press in on me, trying to take the oxygen out of my lungs and the hope out of my heart—not intentionally, of course; it was just the paradigm they lived in. There wasn't much talk of how the mind influences the body, but I knew it did, so I harnessed that power with every bit of energy I could muster.

The struggle with my knee brought to the surface subterranean fears of getting older and becoming less physically capable. I wondered where the line was between what I *thought* I could do and what I could *actually* do. I knew that my body was less flexible than it used to be because of my attempts at twisting asanas in my yoga practice, but that could be attributed to lack of recent practice instead of a true lack of range of motion. These questions wandered into my mind demanding attention, but the answers were not easily located.

The Starting Line

The day before I was scheduled to get the MRI results, I declared to no one in particular that the MRI was going to show that nothing was wrong. I imagined the doctor saying in a puzzled voice, "This shows no evidence of a torn meniscus." Just like Schrodinger's cat, who was both alive and dead inside a box until the box was opened, my meniscus was both torn and whole until we actually looked at the MRI results. Both options existed as a possibility, so I decided to choose which one I wanted to experience. The answer was clear.

I asked my husband to come with me to the appointment. I wanted a witness. I was nervous as the orthopedist brought up the images of the MRI on the computer screen. He put on his reading glasses, leaned closer, and peered at the screen. He pointed with a pencil to the white line that was my meniscus. "Hmm," he murmured. "There's definitely something, but I can't see a tear." I perked up. He pulled up the radiologist report and translated the medical language. "The radiologist doesn't see one either. I'm not sure what's going on. Just take it easy, and see what happens."

I exhaled. The scene played out just as I had imagined it, and I mentally skipped out of the office. My knee was still tender, but I was going to fix it. Somehow.

Chapter 2

Getting Back on My Feet

*Never let a stumble in the road
be the end of your journey.*
—UNKNOWN

When it comes to nontraditional healing arts, I am a cautious believer. I do believe that we are made of energy patterns that direct our physical bodies and that our thoughts directly impact this energy.

Energy healing holds that we must first address the energy body and then physical results will follow, but I had to wonder if a person waving their hands over me with their eyes closed actually knew a process that could help. I also wondered if energy healing would not work on me because I was a cautious believer. It was easier to believe in the process when I read it in a book than when I saw it in person. Like Fox Mulder on the X-Files, I wanted to believe.

Despite the good news from my orthopedist, my knee was still tender, and it hurt when I attempted

Outrunning Age

to run. I meditated and continued to visualize myself running easily without pain, knowing that the more I held that image of myself, the more likely it was that I would connect with a way to bring it about. Intuitively, however, I knew that I needed physical help. Meditation and visualization alone weren't going to do it. I envisioned myself like a radio transmitter, sending out an invitation for that as-yet-unknown assistance. My job was to let the Universe know what I needed and then be open to allowing it to show up, even if it didn't look like what I imagined.

    I had been receptive to energy healing for a long time. My readings through the years had shaped my concept that we humans have both physical bodies and energy bodies, which are composed of life force, or *prana*. Years before, I had struggled with a nasal spray addiction that had been completely alleviated with only three sessions of acupressure. I was open to the idea that the pathways and energy centers of my body, sometimes referred to as *chakras*, could be cleared by a practitioner, which could then create a path to physical healing.

    While I was thrilled to know that my meniscus was not torn, I was still in pain. The pain clouded my thinking at times, raising little flurries of fear thoughts that occasionally darkened my mood. I well knew how my thoughts created my reality, and thought that trying some form of energy healing could help me stay positive while I healed physically.

    My friend Shruti had told me about a course in pranic healing that she was taking and really enjoying.

Getting Back on My Feet

I did a Google search and found this description: "Pranic Healing is a highly evolved and tested system of energy medicine developed by GrandMaster Choa Kok Sui that utilized prana to balance, harmonize and transform the body's energy processes. Prana is a Sanskrit word that means life-force. This invisible bio-energy or vital energy keeps the body alive and maintains a state of good health." This description aligned with my beliefs about my body's energy and physical makeup. I emailed Shruti asking for more information. She quickly replied:

The principle of pranic healing is simple: there is either a depletion or an exaggeration of energy in one or more chakras that is causing discomfort or disease in the body.

Using certain hand rotations and a lot of healing intentions, blockages, depletions, or excess energy are extracted from the troubled area and replaced with a dressing of clean, green, healing energy. Healing can occur instantly or take a few days or weeks.

"I know your knee is still hurting," Shruti said the next time we spoke. "We have a free healing session every Wednesday. Would you like to come?" I knew energy healing could work even if I didn't completely understand it. My deep inner voice immediately said *go!* So I did. I was optimistic but not sure what to expect.

Prana Boost

I had few expectations when I went to the session, but what I didn't expect was to see an old friend. I had met

Outrunning Age

Mike almost twenty years earlier, in a class on spiritual development. I liked his sense of humor, and I had been his practice client when he was just beginning to learn energy healing. I relaxed at seeing him. I learned that he was now a pranic healing practitioner, and since I was one of the group who was dealing with chronic pain, he offered to work on me.

The room was filled with fifteen people, ten attendees and five practitioners. After a warm welcome and a meditation, the pranic healing session began.

Mike asked me to get comfortable in my chair, take a few deep breaths, and relax. "Where is your pain?" he asked. I pointed to my knee. He then proceeded to make sweeping motions with his hands and arms. "I'm feeling for congestion in your energy field, and this helps to align your energy and get it flowing again." He periodically flicked his hands toward a bowl of salted water. "What's that for?" I asked. "When I shake the energy into the bowl, the water traps it and then the salt breaks it down. I love you, but I don't want to take your stuff home with me," he added with a grin. No, we wouldn't want that, I agreed, and relaxed into the chair for the next forty-five minutes.

After the session, Mike asked me what my pain level was. It was hard to tell if the pain was any less, but I was certainly more relaxed. As I looked into his caring face, I so wanted to tell him it was miraculously better—but it wasn't, and I couldn't lie. I told him I wasn't able to tell the difference, and he offered to do another session.

Energy healing isn't about instant relief. I saw it as

shifting the energy of my body enough so that physical healing was possible, whether or not Mike was the person to achieve that. The mystical part of me was open to energy, and the practical part of me knew that physical healing could benefit from physical manipulation, too.

After the second pranic healing session with Mike, my knee pain did indeed lessen, yet I still intuited that something was physically out of whack. I had gone the traditional medical route with my orthopedist and had ruled out surgery, so perhaps it was time to look into a different approach. I still felt that my knee could be healed, despite the pain I felt during my attempted runs.

Healing Hands

A few phone calls led me to a physical therapist named Paul. I liked him right away. During my examination, he narrated to his student trainee what he was finding. He twisted and turned me on the exam table, then asked me to sit up. He placed his hands gently on my knee, squinted, and said, "Your patella is rotated and torqued. That probably happened during your one-legged squat. Don't do those any more," he said with a smile. *No kidding*, I thought. He continued, "As we age, our ligaments don't bounce back the way they used to." As if I needed a reminder. "I'm going to put your patella back where it's supposed to be and tape it up. Leave the tape on for four hours. Come back and see me in a couple of days."

If there is such a thing as healing hands, Paul had them. By the time he finished taping my patella back into its proper place, my knee was already feeling better. I just had a slight residual soreness, like an aftershock of the original pain. I felt that I had finally found the physical help I knew my knee needed.

Once I got home, I continued visualizing running easily and pain-free. I requested that my body and nervous system rewire itself back to health. More tape and a few sessions later, my knee no longer bothered me. It had worked. I was still careful during short runs, alternating between running fifty yards and walking, but I was relieved to see that I was going to be okay.

I said goodbye to my fear that I had run for the last time, and bought myself some new running shoes as motivation.

Chapter 3

Running The Beast

She was powerful, not because she wasn't scared but because she went on so strongly.

—ATTICUS

"You should do Beast for a Day," Brandon said. My nephew was thirty-six, a Spartan racer, a Tough Mudder, and a one-time marathon finisher. His life mission was to prod everyone into doing more than they thought they could.

"I don't know; I hear The Beast is pretty rough," I said. The Beast was an ungroomed mountain bike and hiking trail in the historic town of St. Francisville, a community just north of Baton Rouge. Unlike the flat terrain in Baton Rouge, St. Francisville had inclines and gullies that offered a more strenuous workout for we flatlanders.

Beast for a Day was a trail run put on by ultrarunner Walker Higgins, and runners could choose to run one 5.6-mile lap through the woods or as many laps as they could finish in three-hour, six-hour, and twelve-hour categories. Brandon had signed up for the twelve-hour. While the idea of doing a race was intriguing, I could also easily imagine reinjuring my knee. I knew that the trail wound through the woods, snaking between water oaks, pine trees, and magnolias, and offered a chance at the peace that comes from being in nature. But trees have slippery leaves and roots—sneaky obstacles to unaware runners. I didn't want to revisit the weeks of ache and rehab.

"Just do it, Melinda. You're in better shape than you give yourself credit for," Brandon said. I wasn't sure I was ready to risk finding out if he was right. What if I slipped on a wet trail and injured my knee again? Many imaginary scenes flowed through my mind, but I had to ask myself if I was unnecessarily giving in to my fears. Good preparation and a measure of caution might make it work.

After my knee was healed, I gradually worked back up to run-walking four miles at a time. I knew The Beast course was at least six miles, although no one seemed to know its exact distance. I later learned that this is not unusual in trail running. The idea was, "Who cares? We're out here having fun."

I hemmed and hawed on committing to the run right up to the deadline to enter. I finally submitted my registration and then worried myself silly right up until race day. I armed myself with layers of running clothes so I could shed them as I warmed up. I made sure my thighs were well greased with a lubricant that runners often use to avoid friction burns where body parts rub against each other throughout the duration of a race.

The one-lap group started at eight o'clock in the morning, and my husband, Tom, and I were there at seven, full of nerves. I attempted to look as if I were capable of finishing the race.

After seventeen years of singlehood since my divorce, I figured I would be single for the rest of my life, but then I met a man who made me want to get married again. Tom had divorced after almost thirty years of marriage. He had three wonderful grown children, and was one of the kindest, most supportive men I had ever met. Just shy of six feet tall, with salt-and-pepper hair, Tom is naturally lean and athletic. His exercise of choice tends toward mountain biking, but on this day, his supportive nature had said yes to running The Beast with me. I loved having him as both a running mate and a life partner.

"Go take your 'before' pictures," Walker instructed. We got our race shirts and bibs and then headed off to the photo wall and smiled at the camera. *I don't look as nervous as I feel*, I thought.

As race time got closer, I felt more and more out of place. At sixty and fifty-eight respectively, Tom and I looked to be the oldest runners. Almost everyone else looked to be in their twenties, thirties, and forties, with one or two in their fifties, and all of them fit and athletic. *I hope I don't embarrass myself*, I thought.

My goal was just to finish the race—and to not have

Outrunning Age

to pee in the woods. I had decided to take my ego off the course and aim for finishing last instead of pushing myself to compete with imaginary competitors. *Whew, pressure off.* I also asked Tom if he would run with me in case there were any parts of the course I needed a hand on. I knew there were some pretty steep inclines, and while I was confident going uphill, I didn't want to trip on a root and take a tumble on a downhill.

Finally, it was time to start. My heart was racing. "One-lappers, get ready! Now go!" I told myself to not get all jazzed up at the start and go faster than I was comfortable going. We went single file into the trail head and immediately encountered roots and a downslope. I gradually let almost everyone pass me, and settled into finding my pace.

The runners eventually spread out, and soon Tom and I felt as if we were the only runners on the trail. We heard birds chirping in the oak and maple trees as we ran by, and sunlight dappled the trail. Brandon had advised me to run on the flats and walk up the hills if I needed to, and then power run on the downslopes. We settled into a rhythm, and after a while, I found myself just enjoying the beauty of the woods. *I can do this! I'm doing it!* One, two, three, four miles passed, and we went steadily on, putting one foot in front of the other, our breathing forming the rhythm of the run.

I knew one challenge still lay ahead of me. I had heard mention of the Escalator, which was a boardwalk that spanned a ten-foot drop in elevation over a short distance. I was going to have to traverse what looked like a forty-five degree decline, and I wasn't sure how. The good runners could just run it, but I didn't have the confidence.

I wasn't the only one. When we came around the bend and approached the Escalator, another runner was frozen at the top. We had seen her earlier, and she had wished us a good run as she passed us.

Tom easily ran down the boardwalk and stopped, looking back up at us. I stood next to the woman, unwilling to leave her there while she was in distress. "I can't do this," she said, panic showing on her face. She looked to be in her early forties and was wearing chic black-and-pink running gear—and pearls. She was wearing pearls! I liked that.

"We got you. You can do this!" I said with a confidence that hid my own concern at going down the Escalator. I turned around and imagined myself running down it but decided that the momentum would be more than I could handle. Instead, I stepped onto the boardwalk, squatted down, and slid on my feet all the way down. I turned back toward the woman and saw that Tom had jumped off the boardwalk and reached up a hand to her. She responded by taking his hand, sitting down on her butt, and sliding down the Escalator. "Woo hoo!" We all celebrated.

"Hi, I'm Tiffany. Thanks for the helping hand," she said.

Isn't that the way it is sometimes? We pause at one of life's obstacles and tell ourselves that we can't do it. Then, of course, we can't. Sometimes we need a little encouragement, someone to hold our hand, as we push through the discomfort of our fears.

Tiffany and I ran the rest of the run together, and Tom took off to run at his natural pace. As we ran, I learned that this was not her first race. "When I was growing up, I saw my mother, who was a diabetic, walk only once without a walker," she said. "I didn't want to end up that way myself. I wanted to set a good example for my children."

Tiffany had lost over a hundred pounds over the last few years, and she used races as a way to exercise and stay motivated. While doing obstacle racing and runs, she lost forty more. "You see these compression clothes?" she asked, tugging at her waistband. "They're holding in my loose skin from losing all that weight. I'm having skin surgery soon, and this is my last race before I take time off to heal."

Wow, what an accomplishment! I was speechless. I felt a little sheepish about all the inner chatter I had about my extra thirty-five post-menopausal pounds. I grew curious. "Have you done a marathon?" I asked.

"My mother passed away last fall, but before she died, she was waiting for me at the finish line of my first half-marathon." Suddenly the trail blurred as my eyes filled with tears at how powerful a moment that must have been for them both. "I've run two marathons since, and I have four more scheduled for this fall," she said.

The trail had led us to a creek, and we had to jump off the bank into the shallow water and run in the creek bed until the trail headed back onto the hill. I took my time getting off the bank because I didn't want to face-plant into the water, although I was so sweaty by this time that a plunge would have felt great. We got the giggles as Tiffany splashed alongside me. "When was the last time you played in the water like this?" she asked.

We ran in the creek for about fifty yards and then veered back onto the trail and into the woods. I was excited to see that the finish line was close, only about a half mile away. The trail narrowed, and I told Tiffany to go ahead of me so we could continue single file.

My husband met me at the finish line and pointed me toward the photo wall to take "after" pictures. My face was red, my hair was drenched, and my smile stretched from ear to ear, but I had done it! I was a trail runner; I had run The Beast!

Becoming a Badass

After running Beast for a Day, I declared myself a badass. I was elated and delightfully surprised that I had made it. Doing something I didn't think I could allowed me to put a checkmark in the box of Challenge Your Self-Imposed Limitations. What was next? I wondered if I was capable of doing a half-marathon. If I could do The Beast, maybe I could also do a half, like Tiffany had. The possibility was intriguing, but I knew I would need to learn more before I said yes to a new challenge.

After giving the idea some thought, I decided to take a risk and commit to a half-marathon, even though I wasn't sure what I was doing; I would just learn along the way. I knew that I had to condition myself to go from walking four miles to run-walking the 13.1 miles of a half-marathon—but first, I had to get through the mental noise of chattering self-doubt.

I can't even run one mile continuously. How am I going to do a half-marathon? I mean, if it's a race, you race. If I can't run the entire thing, then I shouldn't do it.

What if I try and can't do it? I'll be a failure. I used to run all the time; why did I quit? I'll just quit again.

On some days, my inner voice took a different tack. *It's hot.*

Yes, it's summer; that's what it's like in Louisiana.

I don't want to run!

I started to think that there was a part of me that deserved acknowledgment. I knew that we sometimes repeat ourselves until we are heard.

I don't want to run!

Heard. *But I want to do the 13.1, right?*

I knew that I wanted the results without putting in the work. I wanted to run across the finish line, arms raised in celebration. Surely one or two weeks of training would get me there, right? The voice in my head told me this was the Way It Should Be, but I knew there were no shortcuts to training up for a half-marathon for the first time—not for me, anyway.

Listening to my self-talk was like listening to a friend who loves you but always gives you bad advice. I knew from life experience that I would live out my mental idea of myself—whatever it was—and that if I gave in to my limitations, they would always define me. I believed deeply that my capacity was greater than my idea of myself. I knew that I could do a little bit more than I thought I could in the moment and that the biggest obstacle was not physical but mental. Self-doubt could always derail me with its insidious whispers. I was going to have to train myself not only physically but also mentally, to learn to ignore the poor advice my inner voice regularly gave me. Managing my thoughts would have to become part of my training routine.

I am a goal-oriented person. Training for a successful half-marathon involved focusing on the process of training instead of the goal of finishing. This was not my natural inclination; I get bored doing the same thing over and over, and crave variety.

I firmly but lovingly started to challenge my thinking. *Being bored is not a terminal event.* Listening to my doubts would be a darn good way for me to derail myself, and I really wanted to complete the half—so I kept running.

Choosing a Training Program

I spun in circles of overthinking how to proceed. Which training plan would be best? Do I try to train up to run the whole thing or to run-walk? Do I train to heart rate or intervals? Do I try to go for pace or just to not die? Christopher McDougall is one of my favorite authors. He is not only a runner himself but also writes about running in a can't-put-the-book-down kind of way. I came across his book *Natural Born Heroes: Mastering the Lost Secrets of Strength and Endurance*. It is the story of the Crete resistance during World War II, including the runners who routinely ran fifty-plus miles a day, day after day, to bring communications to the Allies.

He writes about his visit to a running coach guru named Phil Maffetone, who had trained ultra runners and had developed a specific diet and heart-rate program to help them build endurance through fat-burning. *Fat-burning!* You have my attention, Christopher.

I visited Phil's website (www.philmaffetone.com), where he spells out his approach, the Maffetone Method, using heart-rate training. The first step is to subtract your age from 180, which is the maximum heart rate that an athlete should reach. My heart-rate math was 180 − 57 = 123. Phil says to add five beats per minute if you have been exercising continually, so my final target heart rate was 128.

The burning-fat-for-fuel part involves Phil's two-week food plan, in which a participant eliminates processed carbs and basically eats protein and vegetables. This allows the body to switch from burning mainly glucose to drawing from stores of fat for fuel. The body burns through glucose fairly quickly, but the energy available from burning fat creates endurance. His site offers plenty of recipes that ended up being staples in my overall dietary changes because they were so tasty.

I wasn't sure yet about my willingness to give up some of my food indulgences at this time (wine, cheese, and chocolate, anyone?), so I just experimented with the recipes and committed to Phil's approach to heart-rate training. The part that really appealed to me was the promise that my heart function would become more efficient. For example, if I could run for only thirty minutes before my heart rate went to 128 but then trained consistently, I would eventually be able to run for longer distances or go faster before my heart rate hit that mark. It would be a lovely thing if my heart strengthened instead of weakened as I got older.

Tom and I had both benefited from long-time healthy practices. We met when I was fifty-five, and I knew I would be in this relationship for the rest of my life. We married on October 26, 2013, and I became an instant grandmother of four.

We both had parents who had lived long, healthy lives, and chances were good that if we took good care of ourselves, we would have another thirty or thirty-five years together. We didn't want those years to be spent in doctors' offices and hospitals. We didn't want the other to be burdened with a spouse who was disabled or incapacitated. For these reasons, completing a half-marathon and creating a sustainable exercise program was important to us, and knowing how to improve the function of my heart motivated me.

I needed an overall half-marathon training program. In my search for online training plans, I discovered Jen Miller, a marathon runner who was a writer for *The New York Times*. In one of the first articles of hers I read, she wrote about having been sidelined for months from an injury. I related to that and the fact that she was a female runner, and her story of gradual recovery gave me hope that I could recover well, too. I signed up for her weekly emails and followed her on Instagram (@jenamillerrunner).

Most of the training plans I first came across were oriented toward runners rather than those of us whose approach was a run-walk. I tried to figure out how to adapt the plans and quickly realized I was beyond my expertise. One day, a link in an email from Jen took me to a runner's guide section on *The New York Times* website. I scrolled down to the section on beginner half-marathon training plans. Voila! There it was: my plan. One version for runners and one for run-walkers.

The plan was simple, and I liked the way it ramped up mileage gradually, building endurance in a way that I knew would not discourage me by asking me to perform past my conditioning. Best of all, it wasn't overwhelming: Run-walk thirty to forty-five minutes two days per week. Once a week, on the same weekend day of the race, walk three miles as a warm-up and then run-walk, gradually increasing the miles. Alternate every other week with lower mileage.

Two weeks before the race, my highest mileage would be fourteen miles: a three-mile walk followed by an eleven-mile run-walk. The week before the race, I would do a three-mile walk and a two-mile run-walk. I would then be ready for the half-marathon a week later. The longer distances would build up a mile and a half at a time, and as I imagined myself following this plan, I knew it would work for me. *Just finish and try not to die.*

I signed up for the Baton Rouge Beach Half-Marathon, which started a half-mile from my house. The course wound through LSU and around the LSU lakes, where I ran and walked all the time. I was a little worried about what the weather would be on race day, as early December in Baton Rouge was often cold and rainy—but it could also be sunny and seventy-five. I hoped the weather would be friendly, as I wanted as much as possible to be stacked in my favor for my first half.

The training plan wouldn't kick in in earnest until early October, so I spent the summer getting warmed up, running two or three times per week, and experimenting with the Maffetone Method and different types of intervals. I got to the point where I could tell what my heart rate was based on how I felt, without looking at my watch. I was delighted to see that my resting heart rate had lowered from the low seventies per minute to the low sixties, even dropping into the fifties from time to time.

Conversations with more experienced runners were helpful when it came to running gear. If my ultrarunner friends were wearing Altra shoes, then I was going to, too. If they liked Orange Mud endurance packs to hold water for long runs, then I made a quick search on the internet and had one sent one to my house. CW-X Compression Gear made the best running tights for women? Then send me two pairs. I may not be able to do more than eight miles at one time, but I sure looked like I could.

I made a point to do my runs in the morning before I had eaten anything to encourage my body to use its fat for fuel instead of glucose. After a short adjustment period, I could feel my body gradually shifting.

Outrunning Age

I worked on increasing my speed by sprinting from telephone pole to telephone pole, or any other random landmark, stopping well before I had to. It became easier and easier over time. So much of my running at this point was just learning what my body would do and what it struggled with, and I enjoyed seeing improvements. Maybe I could do this after all.

Then it started raining and didn't stop.

Chapter 4
The Flood

*I did everything I could.
There was nothing else I could do.
So let's get on with it.*
—MRS. "B" EDDARDS

*There hasn't been a flood this big since
Noah built that boat.*
—PERCY BANKSTON

My sweet cat stared in at me from the outside window ledge. Her calico fur clumped together in damp spikes, and she looked more than a tad grumpy. Normally she was fine patrolling the yard for mischievous squirrels and keeping the courtyard free of lizards, but not today. *Why are you letting it rain like this?* she meowed. *Make it stop.*

I sighed and replied, "I'm tired of it, too."

It was August 12, 2016, and it had been raining continuously for three days and nights. The soft *drip, drip,*

drip of water off the camellia bushes formed a background to my thoughts. The constant rain was seriously interfering with my running. I pulled up the weather website once again to check the radar; perhaps there would be a break in the rain long enough for me to get a couple of miles in. What I saw startled me.

Could this be right? I thought. The animated radar clearly showed a pattern of what looked like a tropical depression, slowly rotating in place over Baton Rouge and the surrounding areas. It stretched for miles, and was brightly colored with rain. We normally get afternoon thunderstorms at this time of year, bands that start in the Gulf of Mexico and travel northeast. But this—this was odd. I had seen many of these depressions throughout my years of living in Louisiana. They infuse hurricane awareness into the locals' DNA. What I was looking at was the pattern of an incipient hurricane—over land. I quickly pulled up the ten-day forecast and saw rain and thunderstorm icons stretching ahead; there was not a sunny day in sight. Maybe I should just run in the rain. At least I wouldn't sweat as much. Instead, I grabbed my phone and a towel and opened the door to my courtyard. I dried off the cat as best as I could, and took a video of the constant rain and the saturated ground.

Saturday mornings are Tom's and my time to get a leisurely breakfast, then head to the downtown farmer's market. As we finished breakfast at seven o'clock the next morning, I said, "Let me call Mom. I want to check if the river is up."

The Flood

My mother had lived in her home in a cul-de-sac in neighboring Denham Springs for forty-five years. During that time, the town had experienced flooding twice from the Amite River, which borders the town's western edge. The river was located three miles as the crow flies from my mother's house. I wasn't too worried, as when the river floods, it usually crests far from her home, but I thought I had better check just in case.

"Hey, Mom, do you see water yet?" I jokingly said.

"No, but let me look over the back fence to see if it's close," she replied. I realized she was concerned, and was relieved when she said all was clear. We were all a little antsy at the nonstop deluge.

"Okay, great, if something changes, let us know." I cleared up the breakfast dishes and headed back to get dressed. The phone rang again about twenty-five minutes later. It was my mom again, and the tone in her voice rattled me. "Melinda, come get me. The water is up to the sidewalk and rising."

"Get your medicine, valuables, photos, and clothes, Mom. We'll be there as soon as we can." I took a deep breath as I realized we weren't going to the farmer's market.

I hung up and thought—in the same tone I would wonder what to wear to an audience with the Queen—"Hmmm . . . just what *does* one wear to a water rescue?" I knew that my goofy thought was simply a hedge against the anxiety that was rising as fast as the water. No time for that; use humor instead. I took another deep breath and braced for the unknown.

I thought about what clothes I had that were okay to get soaked. No way was I going in a swimsuit, nor was I looking forward to sitting in wet clothes that would take forever to dry. *I know!* Running clothes, of course. They were designed to get wet. I quickly changed into my running shorts and a tank top, grabbed some water shoes and a raincoat, and headed for the door.

Rescuing Mrs. B

While Tom and I were making our way down I-10 to the Denham Springs exit, the tropical depression I had looked at the day before was busy dumping what would end up to be nineteen inches of rain in Baton Rouge and an astonishing thirty-one inches in the small town of Watson, Louisiana, just north of Denham Springs.

The Amite River was rising by the hour, overflowing its banks and spreading rapidly. By the time we reached the overpass of the exit, I glanced off the bridge to see that the main road into town was completely underwater and that our usual way to Mom's house was blocked. There was brown swirling water for as far as I could see, capturing vehicles and invading buildings. *Oh crap*, I thought. *This is going to be really bad.*

My phone was blowing up with texts from friends wanting to know if we were okay and social media posts telling which roads were blocked and which were still open. We inched our way along in the increasingly heavy traffic until we made our way to the edge of the still-rising water. We were one block from the entrance to my

The Flood

mom's street. I leapt out of the truck and shouted at Tom to find a place to park. We were next to a church, and the parking lot was already filled with kind neighbors with boats who were setting up a rescue brigade. Fortunately, Tom had the presence of mind to note that the water was still rising and so moved our truck around the block to higher ground.

I scouted the situation. The water was up to my knees, and I had a death grip on my phone, careful not to lose my lifeline to my mom. I waded out into the intersection to flag down a passing bateau, a flat-bottomed aluminum boat that was a fixture in every other backyard in Denham Springs. Thank goodness for all the fishermen in Louisiana; those boats were coming in handy today. I had promised my friend Kristin that we would also get her dad, who was elderly and on oxygen and who lived across the street from my mom. *Call him and tell him we'll be coming for him*, I texted her. But first, I had to get there.

"A rising tide lifts all boats," so the saying goes. Baton Rouge had had its share of strife in the last six weeks. First, a young black man was shot by two police officers when they thought he was armed. Two weeks later, as the city was starting to settle down, a mentally ill military veteran took revenge on policemen by shooting six of them in his own version of making a point. Conversation about race emerged everywhere, and blacks and whites mourned losses together. Blue lives mattered. Black lives mattered. Right now, water was mattering. A lot.

Outrunning Age

Water is an equal opportunity destroyer. It is insidious, with superpowers that allow it to enter the smallest of openings and wreak mad havoc in numerous ways. It swells things, destroys surfaces, and gleefully carries toxic chemicals along with it, swirling and sneaking into places where it is not supposed to be. I and hundreds of new evacuees were standing out in the middle of it. I tried not to think about what my skin might be absorbing and focused on how to rescue my eighty-five-year-old mom and not fret about all my other family members who lived nearby.

While I waited for an available boat to bring its cargo of people to high ground and return for me, I watched the parade of people go by. White, black, old, young. A dog in a floating Styrofoam ice chest being towed by a young boy. Families slogging through the rising waters, holding precious belongings stuffed into garbage bags.

I appreciated Louisiana culture at that moment. Everyone was calm and orderly. A couple of people had set themselves up as traffic directors, guiding people on foot into the back of a pickup truck to be ferried to a nearby church on high ground. This was my community, and helping neighbors was deeply embedded in our DNA.

My phone buzzed for the hundredth time. *Who is it now?* I could feel my adrenaline rush. Maintaining calm was becoming a challenge. *Deep breath.* Oh, it was Kristen, with an update on her dad.

Dad was just picked up by boat and is being taken to Northside Baptist, she texted. *Can you pick him up there,*

The Flood

please? Please let me know you got this message. Northside was where we were being staged, so I quickly glanced around.

Looking for him now. Deep in water. I didn't see him, so I waved down a passing boat and asked if they could take me down the street to Mom's house.

The boat was manned by a father and son. The son asked, "Where is her house?" I told him, and the father said, "That sounds like Mrs. B's house." Astonished that he knew her, I responded, "It *is* Mrs. B's house!" He took a second hard look at me and said, "Melinda?" It turned out we had known each other years ago, and he and Mom now went to the same church. I was grateful that Mom would see another friendly face when we came to get her.

I pulled out my phone and videoed our trip down the street, my camera recording the water, which was already three feet up the sides of the houses and waist deep in the road.

As we were launching, Tom waded up and got in the boat, and the four of us motored down Mom's street, up the driveway, and floated right up to the back door. As we pushed the door open, we were caught in a gushing torrent as the water outside rushed to equalize with the water level inside the house. The recycle bin near the back door tipped over in the surge, and our steps inside the house were accompanied by a couple dozen empty aluminum cans. I had a sudden irrational urge to collect them and throw them back outside because cans aren't supposed to be loose in the house.

Outrunning Age

My mother was born in 1930, in a house without electricity or running water, in rural Denham Springs, Louisiana. Her family ate the food they grew, and collectively developed a pragmatic resilience about life's challenges. This day was no different. My mother, all five foot one of her, had calmly packed suitcases, and when we arrived, was valiantly trying to put her most recent batch of homemade jellies up on the kitchen counter, hopefully high enough to save them. We collectively sloshed in, grabbed her things, and loaded her into the boat, floating in two feet of water outside the back door.

Odd things caught my attention. The electrical outlets were under water, yet the floor lamp was still on. I wondered if we could be electrocuted. Why was the electricity still on when the whole town was underwater? One of life's mysteries I never did resolve.

"Wait, I have to lock the door," Mom said out of habit. "I don't think it's going to matter, Mom," I replied as we putt-putted back down the driveway to the street and headed to high ground.

I kept a cautious side-eye on my mom to see how she was handling the situation. Ever pragmatic, she offered, "There was nothing more I could do. I did all I could. Let's just deal with it." She was acceptance personified. No drama, just eighty-five years of dealing with life head-on.

Difficult things happen to all of us. People we love leave too soon. Accidents happen. Our dreams don't come true. In my mother's example, I saw that what is important, what is under our control, what shapes our

The Flood

approach to life is how we respond to what happens. This is not a skill that sprouts fully developed at the first of life's crises. Years of developing resilience had taught Mom the futility of resisting what is, and her response impressed me. Her house was underwater. Okay. There was no, Why me? no, How could this happen? only, I did all I could do. Let's get on with it.

As we develop effective responses to what happens in life, we receive a few dings and bruises along the way. We have to focus to develop skills that serve us. This doesn't mean that we won't grieve or feel our losses; it means the way we look at what happens can help us move through it and not get stuck in the raw places. Therapy, workshops, books, and wise friends can help, and age and insight can bring a certain amount of grace. I was grateful for it in my mom that day.

We located Kristen's dad, Mr. Miley, at a nearby church, and loaded him up into the truck with us. It took two and a half hours to get home, a trip that normally takes twenty-five minutes. We spent a harrowing thirty minutes on the interstate, creeping along in rapidly rising water, hoping we could get through before the water made the road impassable or the battery on Mr. Miley's oxygen tank gave out.

Funny, the things you learn in the middle of a disaster. While I was fretting about needing to pee and hoping we would make it to dry ground before the need became critical, I overheard my mom and Mr. Miley talk about my parents' wedding. Mr. Miley had been their pianist. I had known my mom my whole life and never knew that.

Outrunning Age

We were stuck in traffic that was funneling from five lanes to four and on down to a single lane, where we all continued to creep through the rising water to get to the higher part of the interstate. I distracted myself by attempting to Facebook live for the first time. In the resulting video, we looked like we were driving through a swimming pool filled with floating cars and brown river water. A news clip I saw later that night revealed that had we been only fifteen minutes later, we would have spent the night on the high part of the road, in between the flooded areas where the water would have drowned our vehicles had we tried to get through it. I don't know what we would have done about that oxygen machine's battery.

We dropped Mr. Miley off to his grateful daughter, and when we finally arrived at our house, the enormity of the change hit me. My eighty-five-year-old mom was temporarily homeless, and Tom and I had a new roommate. Forty-five years of memories in her house were washed away in a matter of hours. I was so sad for my mom, and my emotions overflowed. "I'm going out for a run," I said, and headed out into the neighborhood. It felt good to release the energy of the day, my tears mingling with what was left of the rain. I didn't yet know how well my half-marathon training was about to serve me.

Chapter 5

Mud and Mudders

*My barn having burned down,
I can now see the moon.*
—MIZUTA MASAHIDE

Drowned history greeted me as I turned onto my mother's street a few days later. Each house had a growing pile of wet and no longer useful items out front. Furniture drowns, too, I learned. As it dies, it swells. Drawers stick. Laminate loosens. Wood splits as it gives up its former form. *Wow,* I thought, *aging is the same thing. We give up our former form, as well.*

My mom's house no longer looked the same. Drowned furniture sat out at the curb, walls were stripped of sheetrock, and puddles of water shimmered on the concrete floor. A carpet layer in the 1970s was so conscientious that the padding glue was still holding strong forty-five years later.

Once the water leaves, it doesn't leave all the way. Where rain and river water have mixed with the liquids

Outrunning Age

of civilization, a smell remains that clearly marks the territory as definitively as a stray cat that repeatedly sprays. In the days after the flood I sometimes looked around, startled; I imagined that smell even when it was not there.

For three days I dreaded the moment of re-entry to Mom's house as we waited for the water to subside so we could return and assess the damage. I knew the destruction was going to be bad, and I was concerned at how Mom would respond at seeing the life she had built with her husband and family lost in the space of hours.

She was a trooper. We backed off to let her be the first one to enter the house. I held my breath, partly due to the musty smell left behind by the flood and partly to brace myself to support her if she broke down.

Tom had to help push the door open, as the doorway was blocked by a mixture of wet things—cookbooks, their pages swollen open; the floor lamp that we had left burning when we rescued Mom; and those damn cans from the recycle bin. We gingerly stepped into the house, feet squishing with each step, and I glanced at Mom's face as she looked around. After a long pause, she said, "Okay, let's get to work." *Whew!* I released my breath. It was going to be messy, but it was going to be okay.

My Facebook post that day says it best: *It's been a long day. Honestly, I'm not sure where to start to write about what it's like to walk with your mom into the house where she has lived for the last forty-five years, knowing that five feet of water flowed through the house for thirty-six hours or so.*

Mud and Mudders

Furniture is supposed to be obedient and stay where it is put. In a flood, furniture and appliances get curious and visit other rooms. Nothing is where it is assigned to be, and things that are supposed to be dry are wet. Very wet. And squishy.

I discovered that it is fun, in a weird way, to pull up wet carpet and knock holes in the walls with a pickaxe for water to drain through. I'm normally so well-behaved. The mess is overwhelming, really, and our team of my mom, my husband, my niece and her husband, and me had to meet at regular intervals to make a strategic plan for the next hour. There was just so much to handle, and at some point, the surreality makes the brain take a vacation and go away for a while. Logical decisions can sometimes be tough when you're looking at a wet pile of photos of yourself as a child.

Mudders to the Rescue

Shortly after I ran Beast for a Day, Brandon added me to a Facebook group called BTR (Baton Rouge) Mudders, which was composed of obstacle course runners, trail runners, marathon and ultrarunners, and Spartan racers. "I met all these guys through Tough Mudders and races," he said by way of explanation. "You'll like them. They are very encouraging."

As I lurked in the group, reading their posts and seeing photos of medals around many necks, I felt quite out of my league. These were the people who came in first in their age group, and many were top-ten finishers in any competition they entered. But the tone was teasing and supportive, and I could tell that they simply enjoyed friendly competition. I also liked that the group comprised men and women in almost equal numbers, and I began to regularly "Like" posts and comment with WTG (way to go) when someone posted that they had just set a new personal record or medaled in a competition.

On day three of the flood cleanup, ten of the BTR Mudders showed up to Mom's house en masse to show support for Brandon in response to his call for help for his grandmother. The group enthusiastically tackled the cleanup task as if it were the ultimate obstacle race. They went through the house like well-muscled bulldozers, turning the cleanup into mini-competitions.

"Let's see who can take all the baseboards off the fastest. I'll bet it's me. Go!"

"You're such a wimp, I'll bet you can't pull that kitchen cabinet off the wall by yourself."

Piles of sheetrock, soggy insulation, and bedraggled furniture were no match for the Mudders. I watched in amazement as a fit, petite woman hoisted part of a daybed mattress over her shoulder and walked it down the hall as easily as if she were carrying a bag of groceries. I thanked her profusely for donating her time to help us. "We *like* to pick up heavy things and run with them for fun. This is our workout for the day," she said on her way out the door to the growing ruin pile.

I will be forever grateful for everyone who helped us reset Mom's house. The outpouring of time, talent, energy, and resources was humbling. Within a week, the house was stripped to the studs and ready for the

Mud and Mudders

next steps. We were still dazed and numb, trying to mentally incorporate this new and unwelcome reality, but at least the house had been salvaged. My social media post reflected my weariness: *I know I'm a little scrambled by all this flood business. I just tried to unlock my car by using my phone and then wondered why it wasn't unlocking.* #tootiredtothink

My Blog Post, September 3, 2016

It's three weeks after the Great Louisiana Flood of 2016, and I feel a little like a UFO abductee who reports that they can't recall what happened between the time the UFO picked them up and brought them back. I can relate. I think I'm a #LAflood abductee.

Conversations include asking friends if they "got water," shorthand for "Did your house flood? and if so, how are you doing now?" We share stories from the frontline of rescuing family members, saying goodbye to treasured items forever ruined, and celebrating when we learn that "the water came up to the back fence but not into the house, thank God."

Twenty parishes, or one-third of the state, have flooded to the point of being declared an official disaster area. Even the governor had to evacuate.

One news story pointed out that there was no looting, no rioting, and that the flood brought out the best in everyone. I saw that demonstrated over and over, in gestures big and small.

An antidote to loss is gratitude and a sense of wonder at what new good things can come out of this monumental change. I discovered that water has its own artistic ability, and what I

thought at first were ruined photos have instead become flood art. Change in life is inevitable, and like water in a flood, it helps us as humans to flow with it instead of resisting.

The worst of the cleanup was over, and I needed a break from the recent intensity. When the opportunity came up for me to experience a bucket list item, I took it. I was going to fly.

Chapter 6

Flying Melinda Wallenda
Crazy Karl's Reckless Daughter

> *The deepest secret is that life is not a process of discovery, but a process of creation. You are not discovering yourself, but creating yourself anew. Seek, therefore, not to find out Who You Are, seek to determine Who You Want to Be.*
>
> —NEALE DONALD WALSCH

The warehouse where the trapeze rigging hung was really big—two, three, maybe ten stories tall. Despite my being overwhelmed by the scale, I liked the way the rigging looked: the net, the ropes, the trapeze, the pulleys, and the platform where I would either make friends with my fears or be diminished by them. I was relieved to see that the rigging looked impressive, strong, safe. I felt a whisper of *this is something that not everyone can do.* I liked that feeling, too. I hoped I would be one of those people who could.

The voice inside my head held a rapid conversation:

Outrunning Age

What if I can't? What if I embarrass myself? So? No one dies from embarrassment, Melinda. Okay, well, worst-case scenario is that I can't even get up the ladder—or that I get up there and freak out.

    I was nervous and excited to find out. What I hadn't expected was that the instructors would put us through ground school first. There was a protocol, which made sense when I thought about it.

    We were cinched into belts with carabiners on both sides. It started to become real when Kelly, the twenty-something instructor, told me to raise my arms above my head and then yanked on the belt strap to tighten it, pushing the breath out of my lungs. I was about to do this!

    I'm not sure where or when the desire to learn flying trapeze started. As a child, I loved seeing the trapeze artists on the television fly gracefully through the air. Occasionally, the Ringling Brothers Circus visited our city, and I got to see them live. I followed the trapeze artists in my imagination. I was enfolded in a sequined leotard, reaching out my hands alongside them, being securely caught by the catcher, and then being welcomed back onto the starting platform to great applause.

    For some reason I don't recall now, while I was in college, a good friend nicknamed me Flying Melinda Wallenda, Crazy Karl's Reckless Daughter. It wasn't until I was in my late forties that I learned there were flying trapeze schools available for we ordinary non-circus people. Perhaps that desire had simmered subliminally for years, percolating until I couldn't ignore it.

Flying Melinda Wallenda

I don't know why it took me another decade to go for it. Being divorced and again on my own had fueled a sense of aloneness that felt a little risky. Perhaps now, wrapped in the security of a loving, supportive marriage, I had psychological safety straps that I knew would catch me if I fell short of my dream.

I looked around at the other women, veteran flyers who were in the class with us, and hoped they wouldn't judge me, because I sure was judging myself enough for all of us. I was the oldest, the tallest, and the only one who had generous extra padding thanks to menopause. I feared that I would embarrass myself by not being strong enough to hold on to the bar. It sure looked easier to throw a five-foot-two-inch, 120-pound package through the air than to do so with a five-foot-nine-inch package that was forty pounds heavier. I had practiced building my grip over the previous two months but was concerned that it wouldn't be enough. I could feel shame stalking the edges of my thoughts, and I was determined not to let it get close enough to derail me.

Breathe. I looked up at the twenty-foot ladder I would climb to get to the launch platform. There were seven of us in the class, and we went in rotation. I was glad I wasn't first, and Tom followed right after me. As per the ground school instructions, I hooked the ladder safety rope to my belt and put my foot on the first rung. *Keep going. Don't look down. Don't think about how the ladder is swaying. You're safe.*

I reached the top of the ladder, and just before I transitioned to the platform, I froze. I would have to let go of the ladder in order to reach out to the platform support. "I'm really afraid," I told the trainer, who was waiting to guide me through my first flight. "Just grab hold of the support, and I'll get your belt. I won't let you fall. I've got you."

As an independent woman, I almost teared up at hearing those words. *I'm twenty feet in the air. I'm scared. I'm vulnerable. Please take care of me!* I felt an intersection of choices in that moment. I could step forward in trust despite my fears and vulnerability, or I could give in and wonder if that would be the way I would face the oncoming years. I could either continue to embrace and expand new experiences or allow the story of "this is how you get old" to define me. I took a deep breath, grabbed hold of the platform support, and stepped into my future. (Hours later I learned that I had leaned into the top of the ladder so fearfully that I had bruised my upper thighs.)

There I was, on the platform, feeling the edges of my nerves attempting to take over the voice in my head. "Breathe," the trainer said, "I've got you." I felt him reach under my belt and firmly grasp it. I took a deep breath and narrowed my focus to what was right in front of me. If there was ever a time to be mindful, this was it. *I'm about to do this!*

I went through the protocol we learned in ground school. Left hand back, holding on to the support. Right hand grasping the trapeze bar. *It's heavy. It's not a hollow pipe. That rough coating on it is really going to do a number on my hands. I hope my grip lasts.* The trainer called, "Left

Flying Melinda Wallenda

hand! Belly out!" and I mentally took the step of trust. I was twenty feet up, both hands on the bar, belly out, leaning forward. I knew that in just moments, I would take a tiny leap and engage the laws of physics, which would then pull me forward in what I hoped would be a graceful arc. *Breathe.* My heart pounded as I held on to the bar for dear life and waited for his command.

"Ready!" I bent my knees slightly and tried not to think about what was coming next.

"Hup!" he said, and I bounced up an inch . . . and . . .

started . . .

flying.

Exhilarating! *Wheeeee!* I could feel the weight of my body pull against my palms. My shoulders were fully extended, and I intuitively moved my feet forward and back in time with the momentum of the swing. *I could do this forever! Flying Melinda!*

After I swung, the instructor told me to backflip and release. It looked easy enough, but my timing was off, and I landed flat on my back without flipping. Well, no problem; it was my first time.

Next, we were going to hook our knees over the bar and swing upside down. Back to ground school we went, and practiced while lying on the mat. *Where do I put my boobs? This is harder than it looks.* Years of yoga had made me pretty flexible, but I wasn't sure I could pull off this maneuver while flying twenty feet above a net.

I was acutely aware of my fluctuating confidence level; if I had had a confidence meter, it would read yellow.

Once again, I had both hands on the bar, belly out, running through the instructions in my mind. "Hup!" I heard from below.

Swing . . . legs up . . . not quite . . . try again . . . uh oh—face-plant.

"Do I have any skin left?" I asked the instructor, showing her the left side of my face where I had tumbled facedown into the net. She peered closely at me and said, "You're good. Keep your eyes on the bar next time. That will help your timing."

It did, but between my boobs being in the way and tiring out, I just couldn't manage this trick. I felt bad that I didn't get it the first time. I knew this was unrealistic, but in that moment, it didn't matter. I remembered a younger me, lighter, more supple, the me who got things the first time. I momentarily became sad that I wasn't what I used to be. I wondered if this was part of accepting the changes that life brings.

I knew that comparing myself to an earlier version of me wasn't going to do my mood or self-worth any good. *I'm just not as fast as I used to be, not as limber, not as strong*, I thought, but that didn't make my trying any less worthy. I booked this class and, instead of making excuses, did something I had wanted to do for a long time. I decided to have a little grace on myself and gave myself an award for "Best Face-Plant."

The other class participants were very encouraging, which also felt great. My fears of their judging me were

Flying Melinda Wallenda

groundless. "You did great! A lot of people take ten minutes to step off the platform, and you just went right up and did it." As I reflected on this, it occurred to me that trying new things had always been a part of my personality. Vulnerability and courage are often partners. Many times in my life I had stepped up and done something courageous, and now I wondered why I so frequently forgot about this part of myself.

I wondered, too, about my motivation for trying this class. What did I think I would get out of it? What outcome was I looking for? Perhaps I was trying to outrun age. Was that the reason I had also committed to a half-marathon? Two things came to mind. The first was that I had always been active and reasonably athletic, trying different activities throughout the years—aerobics, gymnastics, running, weight training, Pilates, yoga, yogalates, and kayaking—so adding flying trapeze to the list really wasn't unusual.

The second thing was probably the most inspiring. My motivation wasn't so much to keep my body young as it was to keep my mind and attitude young, to regularly follow my curiosity into new territory so that my world would expand instead of contracting through fear. Many times it would be simpler to lie back and keep the status quo rather than meet life with enthusiasm and zest.

I have my dad's portable typewriter from when he was at LSU, just after World War II; it was his version of a laptop. I used to play on it when I was a child, and eventually used it to practice touch typing. It is on display in my living room, and I enjoy thinking of how my dad's fingers touched the shiny black keys as he typed out his papers for college.

When I first set the typewriter out on display, it looked incomplete, so I printed out a piece of paper in Courier font that said, "For a long time, she flew only when she thought no one was watching." I thought a lot about that, and used it as a way to guard myself against making decisions out of my fears rather than my courage.

At trapeze school that day, as I swung away from the platform feeling the joy of my body moving through the air, I flew, and it didn't matter who was watching, because I was watching myself.

Chapter 7

On the Run Again

You always pass failure on the way to success.
—MICKEY ROONEY

My race was ten weeks out, and I was running in the Louisiana heat. My feet felt heavy, and I was soaking wet after going only two miles. It was a bonus run day, a day to run outside of my training schedule, and I wanted to run it without any expectations of pace or distance. I just wanted to enjoy myself.

I was running around the LSU lakes. The morning was sunny, the sky was blue, and I was enjoying seeing all the other runners and bikers who were also braving the heat. We were a mix of ethnicities, ages, and sizes, each of us there for our own reasons.

I had just turned around to head back home when I heard someone call my name. I brought my focus from my thoughts to the road and realized it was my nephew, Brandon, who was on a training run of his own. "I can't slow down," he said. "I'm running for time." "I'll pace with you, then," I said optimistically. I reversed course. I knew I couldn't keep up with him for long, as his relaxed training pace was almost twice as fast as mine, but I wanted to see if my interval training had had any effect on my ability to run faster than I normally did.

I lengthened my stride and quickened my pace to match his. I could feel my heart rate speed up, but I was surprised to be able to stay with him. I knew I couldn't keep it up for long, but I was delighted that I could do it at all. We ran without talking for about fifty yards. I wanted to leave some gas in my tank for the run back home, so after a few more seconds I said goodbye and headed back.

Once I returned home, I saw his post about his run and noticed that his average pace was 7:57. Whoa! A 7:57 means a pace of running a mile in seven minutes and fifty-seven seconds. I was pleasantly surprised that I had run that pace for any distance at all. During my summer runs, I had been having a hard time maintaining distance without having to slow to a walk, so I cautiously allowed myself to think I had made some improvement. Five minutes after I saw Brandon's post, he called me.

"You've really been working," he said. "When you turned around to run with me, I didn't expect you to be able to keep up. You're doing great!"

I was making progress, but I didn't know why I had such a hard time believing it. Maybe I was more comfortable feeling bad about myself. Maybe self-criticism was simply a habit. This was a story I wanted to examine. Running for a couple of hours at a time gave the voice

On the Run Again

in my head plenty of time to drum up self-doubts. I knew more training hours lay ahead, and I didn't want to spend those hours in a cloud of negativity. I knew what to do.

The next day, I settled in for a meditation session and asked myself how feeling bad about myself and thinking I couldn't do something served me. I wish I could say insight burst forth from the wisest part of me, but it didn't. Instead, a quiet voice started to whisper to me over the next few weeks, challenging the negative voice that had hogged my inner mic from the day I committed to the race. That negative voice had kept coming around again and again, like a toddler determined to get her way. The two voices inside my head now had an ongoing battle to get my attention. I was curious to see who I would listen to in the end.

I haven't lost weight. I used to weigh less. I can't run.
If I believe this, I'll never try. It protects me from the shame of failure.
I'm slow. Remember how fast I used to run twenty years ago?
So? I'm out running now.
I haven't finished a half yet, so maybe I can't.
I don't know that.

And on and on.

I prefer running without earbuds, as I like to enjoy what is going on in the moment. Music distracts me

Outrunning Age

from checking in with how my body feels. Training for a long race gives a runner plenty of time to hang out in their own head, if they don't run to music. Gradually, I noticed that the quieter voice was getting more airtime. We find what we focus on, and what we focus on grows. What I had been focusing on was what I had lost in the way of youth and fitness. I had been resisting reality. I had gotten older. I had slowed down. So what? It happens. I could only turn time back in my imagination, and comparing my present to my past was a sure way to suffering.

So, I told myself, *I'm going to find things to be grateful for*. Whenever I caught myself in a whirl of self-criticism, I apologized to myself and looked for gratitude. *I am grateful for sticking to a training plan. I am grateful for my supportive friends. I may not be as fast, but I am building endurance.* "You got this" became my mantra.

Even though I still had my doubts about whether or not I could complete a half-marathon, my training became more peaceful. *I got this.* And then I hit an unexpected stumble.

This Can't Be Happening

It was fifteen days before the race, and I was feeling good about my training. I was a little nervous about the next day's training, as it would be fourteen miles—the most mileage I would have ever done in one session. I thought I could make it, but at what pace?

I headed out to the grocery store to get some

On the Run Again

pre-training carbs. On the way to the store, I reflected on how well my training had gone. I had been consistent, yet I still wondered if I was doing it "right"—whatever that meant. I parked, got out, and walked around to the trunk to get my cloth grocery bag. As I reached out my hand to pop the trunk, I felt my right knee torque slightly and then felt a *pop* inside my knee. I felt immediate, excruciating pain.

Oh no! What was going on? Did I just re-injure my knee? The movement was so innocuous that I wondered why it was hurting so bad. I winced at each step as I limped back to the driver's seat, thinking frantically. I thought about manipulating my knee back into place, and wondered if I could recover in time for the race. When I got home, I reached out in a panic to Paul, the physical therapist who had helped me heal my original knee injury.

He got me in right away. The session with him did ease the pain, but he didn't know if I could heal in time to do the race. "Let's see how it goes. Come see me as often as you need to."

Over the next few days, my knee felt slightly better, but I had developed a new problem: insanely painful plantar fasciitis. Every time I put weight on my right foot, my sole felt like someone was hitting it full force with a hammer. I limped through my day, growing ever more disappointed in myself.

Stubborn, I am. I had trained so diligently that I wasn't willing to give up so close to the race. I waited a few more days and decided to chance a long training session one more time. I tugged on my compression socks and felt the pain in my foot ease when the compression kicked in. I bounced around my kitchen a few times to test the pain level. *Not too bad,* I thought, and headed out the door.

The sunlight made dappled patterns on the road as I ran under the live oak trees around the lake near the LSU campus, encouraged by the beautiful, crisp fall day. I slowly made my way around the first curve, heading toward the rodeo arena, when a darting movement in the holding pen caught my eye. I stopped, squinting slightly in the sun. The fox stopped also, looking back at me. We froze that way for half a minute, then she turned away and trotted around the back of the building. I smiled, grateful for life's little gifts and the bigger gift of being able to run.

Once back at the house, I took off my shoes and pulled off the compression sock. Immediately I knew that running five miles that day was a huge mistake: the arch of my right foot throbbed in pain. It was only a few days before the race, and my hopes sank. Unless a miracle healing happened, this was the end.

Do I or Don't I?

I felt like an imposter as I limped into the hotel ballroom where packet pickup was located. The room was filled with athletic-looking runner folks surrounding the vendor booths, where sellers were demonstrating shoes, energy drinks, gel packets, and a variety of products

On the Run Again

designed to catch the attention of runners with credit cards. I had debated about whether or not to even pick up my bib and race shirt. It didn't seem right to get my packet, even though I had paid for it, if I couldn't run the race. Don't we earn the right to wear a race shirt by actually running the race? I had sure put a lot of weighty expectations on myself.

I made my way through the crush to the T-to-Z table, where a man in his fifties sat behind the packet table, smiled at me, and said, "Ready for tomorrow?" I swallowed hard and said, "I have plantar fasciitis and won't be able to do the race. It was going to be my first." As it turned out, he was the race director, and he was full of advice. "Just run anyway. Do you know how many races I've done with injuries? You should do it!"

He was mimicking the critical voice in my head, and the longer I stood there, the more I could feel tears heading toward my eyes. I was already feeling bad about myself, and this conversation was making it worse. I turned around and limped back out to the car, where my husband was waiting. By this time, the tears were flowing down my cheeks.

"I feel like such a failure," I wailed to Tom. "You're injured. It's not your fault. I know you've worked hard at this, but I think it's the right move not to run," he said soothingly. It was just what I needed to hear at that moment.

I woke up the morning of race day and fought back a resurgence of sadness and disappointment. As I made my way into the kitchen for breakfast, I looked outside

Outrunning Age

to a dreary, cold, and rainy day. Whoa! This was exactly the kind of crappy weather that I had dreaded. I suddenly felt a lot better about missing the race. These were not the conditions I wanted for my first half-marathon. Cold I could handle, but cold *and* wet? No way. At my pace, I would have been out in that weather for at least three hours. I could picture how miserable I would have been. Besides, the T-shirt wasn't all that great, anyway.

Chapter 8

Putting My Best Face Forward

Nature gives you the face you have at twenty; it is up to you to merit the face you have at fifty.
—COCO CHANEL

Do what you feel in your heart to be right, for you'll be criticized anyway. You'll be damned if you do and damned if you don't.
—ELEANOR ROOSEVELT

I looked around the perfectly curated waiting room where I sat waiting to see the cosmetic surgeon recommended by my dermatologist. The perfect shade of muted grey-green, the perfectly proportioned modern chairs and sofa, the tasteful impressionistic paintings that subtly said, "We're professional but caring."

I scrutinized the face of a helper at the front desk who brought me a branded-label bottle of water. A friend had suggested that I look at the staff of any cosmetic surgeon's office. If I liked how they looked—natural

Outrunning Age

yet not overdone, no duck lips, no overly Botoxed faces that couldn't move—then that would tell me a lot about how I would end up looking. The receptionist looked like a normal person with normal facial expressions, so I took a deep breath and exhaled.

I was feeling a little nervous, chatting in my head about whether or not a facelift constituted excessive vanity. *It's only a consultation*, I told myself. I didn't know if I could justify the risk or the expense. Would the benefits outweigh the cost? It was my *face*, a part of me that made me, me. I wasn't a stranger to cosmetic procedures, but I wondered if I was at a place in my life where I would regret it if I didn't have a facelift. I had embraced my wrinkles, counting them as part of the learning curve of my life; however, there were definitely some structural changes in my face that I hadn't authorized. I knew that my body would change as I got older, but I hadn't anticipated just how much some features that I had always liked were altering.

For instance, what had happened to my neck? It wasn't smooth and tight anymore. My jawline had followed, softening from the gentle curve it used to be, and squaring up my face in the process. My neck had gotten so wrinkly over the years that I had once taken gaffer's tape to a photo shoot, pulled my neck taut, and hidden the tape under my hair in an effort to smooth out the crepiness. "And jowls? Do I have jowls now?" I howled one day while looking in the mirror.

"Mrs. Walsh," the nurse called, interrupting my reverie. I followed her into a consultation room. She took

Putting My Best Face Forward

my basic information—my age, what procedures I was interested in—told me the doctor would be with me "very soon," and left the room.

I looked around at more grey-green and thought about why I had come. The idea of getting a facelift scared me. It was surgery, after all, and I had read that general anesthesia and older brains weren't always a happy combination. What scared me more than that, though, was getting a facelift and being unhappy with the results. What if I didn't look like me any more? What if I looked "done," or worse yet, like some Bad Celebrity Plastic Surgery meme? I took a deep breath and again reminded myself that this was only a consultation; I wasn't going to be held down and whisked off to the OR without my permission, much less without paying.

Sure enough, the doctor came in "very soon." He smiled warmly as he shook my hand and introduced himself. "What are you here for?" he asked. I told him that I wanted my jawline back, and that I wanted to know what he would suggest. He gently took my face and turned it from side to side, looking at its every aspect.

I took the opportunity to do the same to him with my eyes. He looked a little younger than I was, late forties maybe. Beautiful skin, but there was definitely some filler around the nasolabial lines. I had had fillers and Botox, and had learned that there was a fine line between *whoops, too much* and *wow, just right*. I wasn't sure on which side he fell, but I decided that he had just had it done and was still swollen.

Outrunning Age

When he was done examining my face, he leaned back and smiled. He then outlined the procedure he saw for me: facelift, laser resurfacing, and upper and lower blepharoplasty (eye lift). Initial recovery would take a few weeks and then up to a year for the swelling to go away. Did I have any other questions? I didn't. We shook hands, and the nurse escorted me to the room where I would learn how much all of this would cost.

I knew it wouldn't be cheap, but seeing those zeroes threw me. It covered the surgery, the doctor, the nurses, the anesthesiologist, and the surgery suite. I wondered if it also covered the tasteful paintings in the waiting room. I left full of doubt but glad I had gone for the consultation. At least I had facts to think about instead of letting my imagination take over.

In the weeks that followed, I reflected on why I was considering this procedure. I had said yes to plastic surgery before, having had a rhinoplasty at age twenty-eight after yearning for one all through my teenage years. I had never had second thoughts about doing it and loved how it turned out. I followed that with liposuction a few years later, which I had mixed feelings about, as the results weren't what I had expected.

I was quite possibly trying to find a way to feel better about myself by having cosmetic surgery. When I looked in the mirror, I didn't see "me" any more, and I struggled to find the balance between acceptance of what was and the idea that getting a facelift was the right decision for me. I knew that an external procedure wouldn't fix an internal problem, so I was careful about

Putting My Best Face Forward

discerning my true motivation. I wasn't about to pull the trigger until I was clear.

I had spent many years in front of the camera, acting in small movies, informational videos, and commercials as part of my income-earning activities. I wondered if I would lose work if I *didn't* get the surgery. I pictured myself being cast as the "old granny" and cringing when I saw myself on screen.

If I went ahead with surgery, it was going to have to be a joint project, as I would be out of commission for a few days. "What do you think?" I asked my husband. Tom paused a moment. I could tell he was choosing his words carefully. "I wouldn't do it; it wouldn't even cross my mind. But if you decide it's something you want to do, I'll support you." I relaxed inside. Part of Tom's nature is to look after others, and I knew I would be in good hands. I also valued his opinion on the doctor I would be choosing.

I cautiously mentioned my desire for a facelift to a few close friends to gauge their reaction. Most were my age or close to it, and had had enough aging changes to relate to my desire to do something about it. "You've made your living from how you look for most of your working life, and you take care of your health," one good friend said, "so why wouldn't you take care of yourself this way?" She had a point.

The best reaction came from my mom, who was a healthy eighty-six years old. "I'd get one if I were willing to spend the money," she said. She pulled at her neck, which looked suspiciously like mine. "I'll come look after you afterward," she said. "Just let me know when you're going to do it."

While the first doctor I saw seemed quite capable and had good before-and-after photos on his website, I didn't feel the yes that I wanted to feel, and I didn't feel a personal connection with him. I felt like just another face in the perfectly curated treadmill of procedures.

I reached out to a friend who was a nurse and whose husband had had a facelift a few years before. He looked great, like a better version of himself, and his short hair revealed no surgical giveaways. Ten minutes after talking with my friend, I had a consultation appointment with her husband's plastic surgeon for the following week. I asked Tom to come with me to the appointment.

Dr. Joseph's office was a bustle of energy, in contrast to the curated, muted tones of the first surgeon I had met with. In addition to being a facial cosmetic surgeon, the doctor also specialized in ear, nose, and throat issues. I later discovered that the paintings that were scattered throughout the office were his own work. They were colorful, robust, and very well done. They looked like they were painted with enthusiasm instead of being chosen because they blended with the wall color. I liked that he was an artist, because he going to be sculpting my face.

"Why are you here?" he asked, smiling as he entered the examining room. "You don't need anything." I smiled back, despite my slight case of nerves. I had learned from Dr. Joseph's website that he was in his fifties. He reminded me of the kind of neighbor you would

Putting My Best Face Forward

ask to come chainsaw the limb that fell into your yard during a hurricane. It was a plus that if he had had any work done, I couldn't see it. I liked his relaxed manner as he listened to my concerns.

"I think I need a facelift," I said. "And probably a browlift, too, since my eyes are looking hooded, but I don't want an upper blepharoplasty because that would change the shape of my eyes, and I still want to look like me."

He turned me from side to side, then surprised me by saying, "You had your rhinoplasty done around the late 1990s, didn't you?"

"Actually, it was in 1987, but how would you know?" I responded.

"I can tell by looking at the inside of your nose the approach the doctor used." I felt both indignant and impressed. *Is there something wrong with my nose?* I thought; I had really liked the results. Yet his comment told me that he was paying attention to what he was looking at.

He left the room, and the nurse took photos of me, straight on and in profile. A few minutes later he came back in and pulled up one of the photos. "Let me show you what I see," he said. The software program he used was like Photoshop for plastic surgery. My jawline looked streamlined. My neck wrinkles were gone, and my eyebrows were raised.

"I can't make you look forty, but you will look ten years younger," he said. Another nurse had followed him into the room, and he now introduced her. "Susan had the same kind of procedure you're considering. Take a look."

"Hi!" she said with a burst of enthusiasm. She lifted up her short hair to show me her barely there scars. "See? He does such a great job of hiding the incisions that you can't even tell." Susan was a few years older than I and was a compelling testament to Dr. Joseph's expertise. I was convinced. It helped to see others who had had a facelift, and now it didn't seem like the big deal it had when I had walked in.

I left clutching the printouts of my promised face and an estimate that was more in line with that I expected. The nurse told me that the doctor scheduled only one procedure per day so that he can completely focus on the patient and their recovery. I was impressed, but I wouldn't be ready to commit for almost a year.

I still wanted to see if I could run a half-marathon, so having surgery would interrupt my running routine. I put the doctor's photographs in a file drawer and concentrated on my training.

It was several months after this appointment that I had stepped out of the car, twisted my knee, and knew I couldn't run the half-marathon. A little voice, strong and firm, said, "Screw the race. I can't run right now, so maybe now's the time for a facelift."

A Google search brings up more than half a million facelift surgery videos: neck lifts, twenty-minute facelifts, even do-it-yourself facelifts. Everything I could ever want to see about what was going to happen to my face was right there, waiting for me to click.

Putting My Best Face Forward

I didn't watch any of them.

Don't get me wrong; I have a sturdy constitution when it comes to watching surgery videos. A sort of geeky curiosity takes over, and I become fascinated by what capable surgeons are able to do with the human body. I don't get grossed out, and I have even been in the operating room while surgery was being performed, but it was an entirely different story when the human body being operated on was going to be mine. I didn't want to feel the phantom sensations I knew I would feel on my face if I watched a play-by-play of the surgery I had now scheduled. I decided to turn my imagination to other, more fruitful things—like imagining how happy I would be once I was healed.

The pre-op appointment was three days before my fifty-ninth birthday. Tom and I met with the nurse in a small room filled with more of the doctor's paintings. (He sure was prolific!) The meeting was a rundown of things I had to do, including taking pre-surgery vitamins for two weeks to prepare my body for healing. My blood pressure was a little high, so I had to get on blood pressure medicine to bring it down before the surgery date. I wouldn't want to have a stroke now, would I? The nurse asked if I was able to walk three blocks without difficulty. Well, I told her, I did run a 10K race last weekend; did that count?

I was glad Tom was with me, because I was overwhelmed after a while. I held his hand as we walked back to the car. *I'm really doing this!* I was excited and nervous; I was about to turn back time!

Outrunning Age

When we were cleaning up after the flood, I had come across a photograph of my father's mother. I had had the pleasure of spending a lot of time with her before she passed away when I was eleven. Born in 1896 in rural Louisiana, my grandmother had been a beautiful strawberry blonde before she gradually went whitish-blonde as she aged. I remember her startling turquoise blue eyes and striking smile, and the way she always made a comfortable place for me on her ample lap.

The photograph was a close-up that showed her smiling, the bottom of the frame cropped just below her shoulders. On the back of it she had written, "Here is a picture of my ugly mug." It stopped me short. She was clearly in the grandmother age zone in her photos but was still a lovely woman. Was this how she had thought of herself? I wondered who in her life had given her that message, had seen ugly rather than the beauty of her life experience in her wrinkles.

My grandmother was sixty-two when I was born, and would live only another eleven years. I thought about all the messages that women get through our culture and the media, and how easy it is to compare ourselves to other women. It is so easy to come up short in our own self-assessments.

There is a movement among some women to proudly disdain wearing makeup, embrace their gray hair, and certainly not indulge in cosmetic procedures. From what I understand, the purpose is to accept who you are as you are, and not be something that other people expect you to be as a woman. I have no quarrel with that. We each have the right to choose a way of being that makes us feel like ourselves, that makes us happy with ourselves.

To some people, I might have been vain by going ahead with my facelift. I was okay with the idea that someone might judge me for it. I was fine with being older, I just wasn't thrilled about *looking* older, so I finally decided it was okay to take a big step to address that. I wished I could have hugged my grandmother and told her how beautiful she was.

Off to the Operating Room

Going through the experience of being prepped for surgery was like being wrapped in the fuzziest, snuggliest blanket I could imagine while surrounded by a host of fairy godmothers whose only desire was to take care of me in the best way possible and to make sure that I was comfortable—while wearing a gown that opened in the back, bright lights shining in my eyes, purple lines drawn all over my face and neck, and Valium dripping through an IV.

One by one I met my care team of several nurses, who introduced themselves while they tenderly held my hand as though I was a newborn; the anesthesiologist, who assured me he would watch me like a hawk the entire time; and Dr. Joseph, who came with his purple pen and a reassuring sense of humor. "Did I mention this is my first facelift?" he said with a grin. I stuck my tongue out at him. "You are in good hands," he said, gesturing to the nurse brigade. A few minutes later, I was wheeled into the operating room. Someone stuck a needle into my arm, and everything went blank.

I was knocked out cold for five hours while Dr. Joseph remodeled my face. Waking up in recovery was a bit of a blur.

"She's awake."

"Your husband's here."

I felt someone take my hand, and my husband's voice sounded like gibberish. "Hey baby, you did great," sounded like "hhheebbbby diddlty gosjrot."

My face feels fat. What's pressing on my throat? Let me sleep. "Ssshhhemmmbbpptmble," I mumbled.

I was vaguely aware of waking up again in a semi-darkened room, with Cheryl the nurse telling me that she had taken care of me all night. One of the reasons I chose Dr. Joseph was that I had complete one-on-one care for twenty-four hours, and he wanted to see me daily for four days.

My eyes stung from the internal incisions of the lower blepharoplasty. Cheryl narrated carefully as she approached me. "I'm going to wipe your eyes, now," she said as she gently hydrated my lower eye area. "You just let me know when you need it again."

So smart, these nurses were. Every time one of them approached me, they spoke out loud. "I'm going to wipe your brow." "I'm going to give you a sip of water." "I'm going to adjust your pillow." Being sedated is a very vulnerable situation in which to be. I couldn't communicate in my normal fashion. Hell, I couldn't even *think*

Putting My Best Face Forward

in anything but mumbles. I would have been startled if someone had approached me without my knowing what they were going to do. Even in my drugged state, I sent up a thought bubble of gratitude for the person with the insight to make that approach standard operating procedure.

The door opened and Dr. Joseph came in. He patted me on the shoulder and said, "You did great. It was five hours, but I'm happy with the results." I attempted to communicate that I thought the bandage across my throat was too tight and was impairing with my ability to breathe. It felt like someone had a finger on my windpipe and was pressing on it. I felt panicky and started to hyperventilate, struggling to maintain control as I spoke with him. Cheryl quickly gave me a Valium.

I later learned that the bandage was just fine. The swelling around my platysma muscles—those two ropy lines at the front of the neck in people over fifty—were putting pressure on my windpipe. Dr. Joseph had threaded them up and pulled them tight, just the way I laced up a pair of running shoes. Fortunately, the discomfort subsided after a couple of days.

Over the next four days I lay on the couch, ate pain medicine and chocolate mousse every four hours, and didn't remember much. By the end of the week, I had recovered enough to marvel at the rainbow colors of the bruises on my cheeks and appreciate how all my wrinkles had vanished due to the swelling. I could also appreciate that I looked a bit like Frankenstein's sister, with an added touch of really dirty hair.

Dr. Joseph explained that because of my high forehead, I couldn't have a regular brow lift, as it would make my forehead even higher. The alternative was to make a more natural-looking zigzag incision at my hairline, raise my brows, snip off the extra skin, and stitch it all back in place. The stitches traced my front hairline, around and behind my ears, and around the back of my head. I wondered if Dr. J put his initials in my scalp. There were *a lot* of stitches. I honestly looked a Technicolor mess.

I had chosen Dr. Joseph well, though. When I commented that he had preserved my widow's peak, he said, "I put it where it belonged, in the center." Oh. "And I lifted your nose tip a little."

"How did you do that?" I asked, wondering how it was possible without another rhinoplasty. "Simple. I put a tiny stitch in between your eyebrows, and it pulled it right up." God bless Dr. Perfectionist.

Day by day the swelling subsided, and I finally got to wash my hair. Twelve days after the surgery, I was presentable enough to go out in public. While I didn't post on social media, I did document my progress on my phone, and my expression shows just how happy I was with how the results were turning out. I wondered if anyone would notice, and if they would judge me negatively for what I did. People did notice, but they weren't sure what they were seeing.

"Did you lose weight? You look great!"

"What did you do? Did you get a new haircut? You're glowing!"

Putting My Best Face Forward

My two favorite comments, which are indelibly seared into my brain, came on two different occasions. The first was when I got my hair cut about four weeks after the surgery. Lee had been doing my hair for twenty years, and I had tipped him off at my last styling prior to the procedure. Now, when I walked into the salon, he popped his head up and looked at me closely. "I remember you!" he exclaimed. "I've known you since you used to look this way!" I dissolved into giggles. "Don't make me laugh," I said. "My face still hurts!" His comment reassured me that I still looked like me, only refreshed.

The rest of my doubts evaporated at my stepson's wedding, which took place eight weeks after my facelift. I had hired a professional makeup artist to do my makeup, and my hair was professionally styled. I was still swollen enough so that my wrinkles were faint, yet not so swollen that I looked weird. Everything came together, and I felt beautiful. My husband wore both his tux and his role as the father of the groom handsomely. Everyone in our blended family was present and filled with good cheer and happiness at the union of two wonderful people.

The evening reception took place on a terrace overlooking the Mississippi River. I took a break from dancing to enjoy the beautiful April weather, and walked to the balcony to watch the nighttime sparkles on the water. I thought about how lovely it was to be a part of this family, who had gently reached out to re-form after the divorce that had made my husband sad but ultimately opened the way to me.

Outrunning Age

I loved my new daughter-in-law, and thought she made a wonderful partner for my stepson. Their friends had wound their way into my orbit during the months of pre-wedding parties, and one of them found her way over to me during my reverie on the balcony. I liked her because she was as smart as could be and said what she thought without much filter. This conversation was no exception, and hers was the second of my two favorite comments.

"Ms. Melinda," she said, waving her half-glass of champagne. "You are so hot! You could get any forty-year-old guy you want." She looked momentarily abashed. "Uh, not that you would ever *do* that. But you could!" She waltzed away in search of more champagne.

I smiled, appreciating the unsolicited compliment. I hadn't done the surgery because my self-worth depended on being thought hot, but I appreciated the moment for what it was: a lovely compliment from a lovely person. I also appreciated myself for having the courage to thoughtfully take a big step that was right for me.

Chapter 9

The Year of Being Noncommittal

You have to go wholeheartedly into anything in order to achieve anything worth having.
—FRANK LLOYD WRIGHT

My self-doubts got the best of me for the rest of my fifty-ninth year. While I was quite satisfied with the results of my facelift, I noodled around halfheartedly with the idea of doing either a half-marathon in the fall or the Louisiana Marathon the next January. My reasoning was goofy but made sense to the part of me that remembered all too well the feeling of failure that came from training and then not racing.

I won't turn sixty until February, so I can't do the Louisiana half-marathon this coming January because I'll still be fifty-nine. This was code for *I don't want to feel the disappointment again if I try and can't do it.*

One half-marathon race date after another came and

Outrunning Age

went without my participation. Finally, after the Louisiana Marathon date had passed, I asked myself, *How am I going to feel if I don't honor my commitment to myself to do a half-marathon?* I certainly didn't have to, and my life would be just fine without doing so. It was enough to be able to do the mileage, so I questioned why a race was necessary for me to claim success. If I didn't participate in an official half-marathon, though, I might then see myself as someone who couldn't complete her commitments, who lacked the courage to test where her capacity was. Worse yet, I wondered if I was afraid of giving my best and having it not be good enough. What would that do to my self-worth?

My thoughts returned to how I felt when I watched that sixty-year-old woman cross the finish line. As I checked in honestly with myself, I realized that I would regret not doing the race. I wanted to be that woman who was willing to put in the effort to reach a goal that was important to her, regardless of the outcome. I decided I would go for it. This time, however, I was going to get a different kind of help.

In the Nick of Time

Tom and I had run the Beast for a Day trail run for the second time earlier in the year. I loved running in the woods and yet was a little uneasy about the possibility of a fall. Once again I thought of the roots hidden under slippery magnolia leaves, and tried not to envision the one misstep that could send me tumbling

The Year of Being Noncommittal

headfirst down the path and having who-knows-what break before I stopped. I could feel these fears slithering toward me, capitalizing on all the messages our culture gives us about reining it in as we get older.

I didn't worry about these kinds of possibilities when I was younger, yet I had to admit that my body just wasn't as agile as it used to be. I wasn't about to let this stop me from trail running, but I was more aware of how my thoughts had shifted. I had fallen down a flight of stairs ten years earlier and dislocated my elbow. That had shattered my innocence about getting hurt, so I was cautious but still gave my best.

I was determined to face down my fears with action—but go *splat* I did. The one tumble I took this time around came as I was climbing over a fallen tree. My back foot tripped on a vine as I was bringing it over the tree, and I landed smack on my chest in a pile of sand. *Good thing I have cushions!* I thought. I wasn't hurt, but I sat there and giggled at myself for a few seconds before getting up and finishing the race.

I had gotten off easy that time, but the question kept nagging at me. What exercise could I do that would counterbalance or even reverse the loss of agility and balance that I was already experiencing? The answer came with an order of salsa.

I met a group of friends at a local Mexican restaurant for dinner, and sat next to Karen, whom I hadn't seen in almost a year. "Damn, girl, you look good!" I said. "What have you been doing?" Karen was a year older than I and blessed with thick hair, bright blue eyes, and a youthful face. The last time I had seen her she had been a little on the plump side, but now she looked sleek and healthy.

"I've been working out with Nick, and the scale doesn't really show it, but the workouts and keto food plan he has me on have made a difference. I'm two sizes down."

I immediately got Nick's number and made an appointment for the following week. Over years of trying different forms of exercise, I had learned through trial and error that mentally, I needed to hand myself over to a trainer's guidance (with the exception of running, which I was happy to do on my own). Otherwise, I would start strong, overthink it all, get overwhelmed with which-plan-is-the-best-for-me, and swap the gym for the couch.

While I was waiting for my appointment, I asked Brandon if he knew Nick. "Nick Ortego? Yeah, he's a super fitness guy. Knows his stuff. You'll like him; he's done a hundred-miler." This was good news. Since Nick had trained for and completed a hundred-mile race, he would certainly have the expertise and experience to coach me to complete a 13.1 mile race.

When we first met, I was surprised by Nick's approach to training. I walked into his studio on the first day expecting to work out, but instead, he pulled up two chairs and invited me to take a seat. He looked to be in his early forties, fit and trim, with close-cut light brown hair and a longer beard. He exuded calmness, confidence, and a chill vibe.

The Year of Being Noncommittal

We talked for almost an hour as he asked me questions about what I wanted to get out of working together (regain lost agility and fitness; weight loss would be a bonus). I shared the story of how I had injured my knee by listening to a trainer who pushed me too far.

"I really, really don't want to get hurt again," I said, remembering the angst of my injured knee. "I can't do what I used to be able to, and I'm concerned that someone younger may not understand that." Nick assured me that many of his clients were in their forties and fifties, and I began to relax. He viewed himself as a partner, coach, and encourager, not just a trainer. I liked that he referenced meditation and emphasized how important a mental approach was, in addition to a physical one, when it came to fitness.

On my next visit, Nick put me through a series of physical movements designed to determine where I stood in regards to general ability and overall fitness. I squatted with my arms overhead, stepped back and forth across a low PVC pipe hurdle, touched my toes, lay down and pushed what looked like a blood pressure cuff placed behind my back to measure my ab strength and control, attempted to touch my closed fists behind my back, one behind a shoulder and the other at my waist. Finally, I lay face up at the end of a massage table, my legs dropped toward the ground to see how flexible my hips were.

At the end of the round of tests, Nick told me that my quadriceps were tight, my glutes were weak, and my shoulders were rounded because my pecs and shoulders were tight. "What?" I exclaimed. "I'm a runner! I have weak glutes?"

I had also struggled to keep good form as I squatted, my arms drifting downward and my knees sagging in as I struggled to rise. For a moment, reality crashed into the fantasy that maybe I was physically much younger than my age. Flexibility—yes. Ab strength—not bad at all. But the rest of the results were not as I had fantasized. I took a deep breath and reminded myself that this was why I came—to work with an expert. I therefore reframed these results as a helpful diagnostic; now we knew where our work would be focused. I committed to an hour once a week with Nick, at nine o'clock Wednesday mornings, supplemented by two training run-walks on my own.

Okay! Good start on my running support, but I still was not happy with my weight. I am five foot nine and had been a size six until menopause. *Congratulations, Melinda! You've just had your last period. Here are some night sweats and twenty extra pounds as a reward.* Whose body was this, and what was going on?

Within the space of three years I had gone up almost three sizes and ultimately gained thirty pounds. It had happened gradually, and I lied to myself as the weight went on. *I'm tall; I can carry a few extra pounds. No big deal.* There are only so many times one can do that without reality catching up. I couldn't pretend any more. I was growing uncomfortable in my body. I was now personally acquainted with what a middle-aged spare tire meant, and I felt like the Tin Man, whose joints needed

The Year of Being Noncommittal

oiling. My joints didn't ache, they were just stiff. It was time. I was ready to address my extra pounds for good. I was not confident that I could lose the weight, however. I had worked with two different nutritionists and engaged in a group weight-loss program, all with disappointing results. Having followed the plans to the best of my ability with no change at the end felt terrible. I wondered if I was just going to be uncomfortable in my body for the rest of my life. Maybe I should just accept this is as The Way It Is. After all, having been thin for most of my life, I had no skills to help me lose more than a few pounds.

I swallowed my ego along with a gulp of wine, and looked for someone who had a proven program, who could make all the decisions for me—someone like a trainer for weight loss and, even more importantly, my overall health over the long run.

As often happens, when I get clear and committed about what I want, the answer for how to achieve it quickly finds me. Within a week, I came across an ad in a local lifestyle magazine for Mint Health, a functional medicine program run by a local doctor. I watched a video on their website that described the program, and learned that it was customized to each participant's unique lab test results—not the one-size-fits-all approach that had been unsuccessful for me in the past.

A monitored food-elimination program would teach me how to identify foods that were causing inflammation in my body. This intrigued me, as I knew that inflammation was at the root of many chronic conditions, including excess weight. I knew my body wasn't functioning as well as it could be. I hoped I wouldn't have to break up with cheese, but I was willing to see if I needed to. Some food relationships have an expiration date.

Shortly after signing up for the year-long functional medicine program, I realized I had also signed up for a part-time job of creating new habits. I won't lie and say it was easy; it was overwhelming at first. There were so many things to remember and change. The first and biggest hurdle I had to clear once I started the food elimination program was figuring out what on earth I would have for breakfast if I wasn't eating eggs. One morning I burst into tears of frustration over this very thought.

Over the course of four weeks, I eliminated four foods each week that were known to cause inflammation in the body—common culprits like eggs, dairy, soy, sugar, alcohol, and wheat. In addition, each week I increased my vegetables from two servings to four with every meal. We were encouraged to "eat the rainbow," which inspired me to try vegetables I hadn't been used to eating.

Neuroscience research tells us that any time we attempt to change a habitual behavior, we are faced with resistance from the neuronal pathways that were created and reinforced by the original behavior. These connections were formed over time, and repeated thoughts flow through them swiftly. To change a habit, we have to literally create new brain connections that will allow us to more easily perform the new behavior over time.

The Year of Being Noncommittal

During this transition, we experience discomfort and resistance to change.

My automatic go-to for breakfast was two scrambled eggs with cheese and two pieces of bacon. I found myself oddly emotional when I contemplated giving up these foods, even temporarily. I felt like I was being punished or deprived, and my inner teenager was not happy at all. I was *friends* with my eggs, for heaven's sake.

In a sense, I was going through withdrawal of my old way of being around food, and I grieved the way I had used food in the past for emotional soothing. Stressful day? Chocolate will help. Never mind that it often triggered a surge of guilt for emotional eating, which then inspired a loop of more chocolate, then . . . you get the picture.

For the first two weeks, I told myself that my discomfort was a sign that the program was working. Gradually, as I reworked my eating plan, my body began to respond. My outlook lifted, and I had more energy to do my daily work. I noticed that if I thought about doing a task, I would do it right away instead of thinking, *I'll get to that later.*

My clothes began to get looser, and the stiffness in my muscles and joints eased up. People started telling me my skin looked great. After eight weeks, the scale in the doctor's office showed that I had lost seventeen pounds. My blood pressure had normalized, and I no longer yearned for eggs for breakfast.

After a food re-introduction period, I learned that dairy made me repeatedly clear my throat and that wheat and sugar made me bloated. After tuning in to the effects that cheese had on my body, my desire for it dissipated. What felt the best to me was making a commitment that wasn't easy and then sticking with it long enough to see the payoff.

My personality style is to throw myself intensely into a burst of short-term energy in order to make changes quickly. Some people thrive on consistency and routine, but that's not my nature. I knew that completing a half-marathon would mean sticking to a food and training plan for longer than a week, and I was delighted to discover that the success I felt at my body's changes were enough to help me let go of my impatience and continue toward my goal.

Losing weight helped my running, too. Between eating in a way that supported my body's function and Nick's diagnostic exercise plan, I was running easier and building up endurance. As promised, the Maffetone training combined with my eating plan kicked me into ketosis, when I was burning fat for fuel during training. I could easily do a run-walk training of nine or more miles before eating anything without crashing or immediately needing to nap. The amount of weight I had been carrying around hit home when Nick handed me a fifteen-pound kettlebell and said, "Imagine running with that. That's what you've been doing." It shocked me and inspired me to continue.

One day while on a training run, between one step and the next, my body unlocked. I had unconsciously been holding my shoulders and hips tight, and suddenly,

The Year of Being Noncommittal

my muscles loosened up and my form changed. My posture shifted at that point also, shoulders back instead of rounded, my head high. My stride lengthened due to my hips releasing, and it hit me that I hadn't felt this way while running for many years.

I still had weeks of training to go, and this time, I was going to make it.

The Mental Challenge

"Hey, I need some help. Do you have time to talk?" I reached out to Brandon, who had taken on the role as my unofficial coach and chief motivator. While I was recovering from various injuries, he had worked his way from full marathons to ultra races and was currently training for a hundred-miler while also running obstacle course races and the occasional trail run. I admired his commitment and consistency in training, and was grateful to have someone in the family whom I could call on for training advice and encouragement.

"I'm feeling really crappy about training again," I told him when we connected. "How can I be motivated when the half-marathon I want to run will be handing out awards to the winners before I even finish?" My ego was in full attack mode, firing out excuses, doing its best to keep me from attempting something that would disappoint me again. I knew what that voice was doing, but it still felt real.

"Melinda," Brandon said, "I wish you could come out to one of these ultra races, where people are trying

Outrunning Age

thirty or sixty miles for the first time. They don't know if they can hold up for the whole race, but the point for them is to try. You're doing something for the first time. Just make it your goal to train well and finish. Then the next one will be easier. Look at this race as your ultra." I felt better after I hung up from talking with him. I had never looked at my training that way: this race was my ultra.

I first met ultrarunner Walker Higgins when we ran Beast for a Day, and got to know him a little better during the flood cleanup. His take on running a hundred miles or more at one session helped ease my concerns. Walker said that when people first learn about ultrarunning, they can't get their minds around it. He pointed out that for the runners, though, it's a progression, and that consistency is key. We all start somewhere, after all.

I could relate to this. Before I started training, I would imagine driving thirteen, twenty-six, fifty miles in a car, and would think, no way could I do that on foot. What I overlooked was that without training, of *course* I couldn't do that. No concert pianist starts out playing a Rachmaninoff concerto. They start small and work their way up, putting in practice hours until they reach performance status. Running training was no different.

One of my first runner friends was Andy Hauck, who had been running at a 7:30 per mile pace, six days a week for thirty years. Another friend, Lorraine Moller, was a Olympic bronze medalist in the women's marathon and a Boston Marathon winner. Through Brandon I met many runners who were veterans of very long

The Year of Being Noncommittal

distances and who usually won or placed due to their talents and commitment to training. Every one of them had moments when they tried more distance than they ever had before, and used the experience to learn how to do it more effectively the next time. And the next.

I realized I had been comparing myself to others without taking the entire picture into account. I thought of a meme I saw the other day: *Don't compare your raw footage to someone else's edited version.* I was starting to see that the physical part of running was the easy part. Any running goal involves regularly committing to it and addressing the obstacles that we put in our own way. I was glad I had my nephew to help talk me over my mental hurdles.

All that was left to do was to follow the rest of my training schedule. For the first time, I could see myself crossing the finish line.

Unexpected Encouragement

"What's my stroke?" I asked Tom. We were talking about how, as a caretaking personality, he sometimes struggles with discerning between when someone truly needs his help and when they don't but they know they can manipulate him into helping. This often led to his feeling taken advantage of or being overextended. From the point of an outside observer, I could see that what often stroked his ego was a need to be needed combined with his pride of being the guy who always knows how to solve problems. I pointed out that this often made it challenging for him to stop doing for others and take care of his own needs. "Would you agree?" I asked him, and he nodded.

I paused and thought a bit. "So, from your point of view, what's mine?" I asked.

"Applause," he immediately responded. "You like recognition for doing something well." I laughed, because I often thought of my inner five-year-old Melinda, who was definitely motivated by, "Good girl! Yay you!"

Yep, my husband had nailed it. I was that little kid who enthusiastically showed off a new skill to any adult within earshot. "Want to see me do multiplication tables?" "Want to hear me play the piano?" "Want to see what I just drew?" My need to not only do something but do it really well started at an early age.

The kindhearted adults in my early life pretended to find me fascinating and piled on the kudos, which served to build my confidence and ignite a joy of learning. I eventually outgrew the need to create on-demand audiences, but genuine acknowledgment of my creative expressions still motivates me.

Tom continued. "You also have a hang-up. Want to hear it?"

Hmmm . . . I did and I didn't, but I trusted his observations. Deep breath. "Okay, go."

"You not only want to race, you want to win. I see that desire keeping you from enjoying yourself at times."

I sighed. Hubs nailed it again. It wasn't mentally easy to commit to training for a half-marathon again. My pace was slow, and the competitive, applause-seeking

The Year of Being Noncommittal

person that I could be knew I wouldn't come anywhere close to placing, so I couldn't use that for motivation.

While the conversation with Brandon had helped me reframe running the half as my personal ultra, I knew I still needed to put in the miles. I didn't know if I was up to it or if I even had enough time left on the calendar to properly train. It was winter on the Gulf Coast, and I knew that we could have beautiful, warm days followed by dreary cold. I was just tentative enough to know that I could get derailed by poor training conditions and, even more, influential and unrealistic expectations on my part. Another reminder to manage my mindset.

I got out my calendar and my training plan and back-timed from the race date. Based on my current fitness level, I determined that I had just enough time to train for the race. The first long training would be a three-mile warmup walk followed by a three-and-a-half mile run-walk at my own pace. I knew I could easily handle that without needing mid-session energy gel or extra water.

Whoops. Then I saw that I had miscalculated the dates. In addition to twice-weekly thirty-minute run-walks, I would have to alternate between long mileage and four- or five-mile sessions every other weekend. Now I was off by one week, so I saw that I would have to do two long-mileage weekend sessions in a row, a six-and-a-half miles one weekend followed by an eight-mile the next. For the latter, I would start with a three-mile warmup walk, then shift into a five-mile run-walk, which was at the edge of what I thought my capacity was.

Outrunning Age

To make the training more complicated, the eight-miler would fall in the middle of a family New Year's Eve get-together on the Florida Gulf Coast, five hours from our house. I took a deep breath and realized that training takes place no matter what, and I really wanted to be ready on race day. I checked the upcoming weather, and packed every bit of my running gear so that I would be ready and comfortable no matter the conditions.

Off we went to Florida for a three-day family weekend that included three grown children and their spouses, seven grandchildren, two grandmothers, two aunts, and one ex-wife and her husband—twenty-one people in all. We were two blocks from one of the most beautiful beaches on the Florida panhandle, and despite the mix of people and personalities, I knew our family time would be harmonious.

I was looking forward to running near the beach. There is something deep inside me that could stare at blue-green water all day long, and the white sugar-sand beaches on the Florida panhandle are gorgeous. I wanted to find an eight-mile path; I didn't want to have to run back and forth on the same two-mile stretch. I asked my husband to ride the beach road with me in our car so that I could map out my route in my mind. As we rode down the road, I tried to guess the distance as we were driving. While I'm running, it is clear to me how long a mile is, so as we ticked off the miles in the car, I was happy that I could envision what it was going to feel like to hit each mile and know that I could make the eight.

The Year of Being Noncommittal

I waved goodbye to the family horde in the rental house and headed out into the beautiful day. The sky was cloudless and blue, the temperature was just cool enough to keep me energized but not so cold that I couldn't get going, and I settled in to do my miles. I decided to not worry about my pace or overall time; I would just keep an eye on my heart rate, and slow to a walk once it passed a certain point.

It was challenging to accept the changes that the years had brought. I weighed more than I did when I first started running twenty-two years before, and I had difficulty running a longer distance without having to stop and walk. This did not sit well with my ego, which expected me to not be bound by the laws of physics or aging. If I knew someone who could run a marathon in under four hours, shouldn't I be able to?

My eight-mile training that morning gave me a lot of time to examine the inside of my head, and I felt at times like I was arguing with a determined toddler who wasn't at all interested in listening to any kind of rationale. Then I remembered something Walker Higgins once told me. "One thing I've never allowed myself to do is say, 'I can't keep going.' I say instead, 'I don't know if I can keep going.' Not knowing is okay."

Self-talk is incredibly powerful. We chatter to ourselves all day long in an attempt to create meaning out of the events of the day. If we lean toward a negative interpretation, we can create limitations by telling ourselves we *can't* or *shouldn't* when there is no good reason to hold ourselves back.

Outrunning Age

From watching older friends, I saw that their default for aging was a shrinking world, either from waning interests or physical limitations, so some of that was inevitable—but I didn't have to help it along. The first time I ran farther than I had ever run before fostered a sense of accomplishment that bled over into other areas of my life. I loved being the person who truly found the idea of an eight-miler possible, because I remembered so many years of being afraid of a 5K. Suddenly, tackling a longer distance didn't seem like such a big deal.

As I ran, I became my own kindhearted adult, cheering on the little Melinda inside. *One mile down, only seven to go! Yay, you!*

You've made it halfway, and you feel great! Don't worry about pace, this is a training run. You got this!

Only two more miles . . . that's nothing; you know that!

I soaked up the sun and the self-generated encouragement, then headed back to the family rental house, hoping there was some lunch still left for me.

I am "MeMe" to seven grandchildren, who then ranged in age from five to eighteen. Collectively, they were nothing if not enthusiastic and encouraging about just about everything. When I walked into the dining area after my run, a chorus of voices greeted me. "MeMe, is it true? You just went eight miles?" I assured them that it was. I was caught off guard when the entire family burst into applause. I blinked back tears as I stood in gratitude for my husband's family, who have embraced, loved, and supported me in the years we have been together. Both the little kid inside and the grown-up MeMe were happy that day.

Later, Tom told me that as we drove my route, it seemed to him that eight miles was a really long way, and he couldn't believe I was about to do it. "Really?" I responded, and realized how different our experiences were of our test trip. Where he saw a long distance, I saw only the possibility that I was capable of finishing.

"And one more thing. Did you put everyone up to applauding for me?"

"Nope," he said, "that was entirely spontaneous. I'm really proud of you."

I savored the moment. Not all of my training runs, or even the race itself, would be as enjoyable as this day was. Having the support and the sweet memory of spontaneous acknowledgment was going to serve as motivation for the rest of the training miles leading up to race day.

Chapter 10

Race Day, Take Two

Nobody who ever gave his best regretted it.
—GEORGE HALAS

Your capacity is greater than your idea of yourself.
—ALAN SIELER

Race day dream: I was at Lorraine Moller's house, and she was heading out the door, saying "Just turn the lock on the bottom knob; you won't need the deadbolt key." Before she left, Andy Hauck came in through the back door. I was glad to see him, as he had passed away in 2012. In the dream, we all chatted a bit about relationships, and then my alarm went off.

I had laid out my clothes the day before, attempting to divine just which layers I was going to be comfortable in for 13.1 miles in windy, damp, thirty-three-degree weather. Training for increasingly higher mileage through varying weather conditions had allowed me to experiment with different combinations of running clothes. Do I wear the layers I would need once I warmed up, or do I wear a jacket for the start and then wrap it around my waist later? Over time, I had figured out what would work best for race day, no matter the conditions. I decided to trust my experience.

I wrapped myself snugly in my aqua polka-dot compression socks, black compression tights (the ones with my favorite color turquoise piping), an undershirt, a thermal shirt, and a black jacket that came down well past my waist. For some reason, my backside always gets cold when I run in cold weather. A seasoned runner friend suggested that I cut holes in a garbage bag for my head and arms, and wear it to block the wind until I was warmed up.

As I walked into the race starting area, I was thrilled by what I saw. So many people! So much noise! So much excitement! *I have to go to the bathroom. Where are the Porta Potties? Remember to slip my hand warmers into my gloves. Find my Mudders friends to take a pre-race photo.* (We are all grinning, and you can't see us shivering.) *Find a spot in the middle of the pack at the starting line to stay warm between the national anthem and the start of the race.*

As I listened to the final notes of the national anthem and looked around at all the other runners, I found myself unexpectedly emotional. I was doing it! I had trained well and knew it. I had run the miles, done the homework, and was about to complete a goal I had set for myself three years prior. In just a little while, I was

Race Day, Take Two

going to be the sixty-year-old woman who was crossing the finish line after running a half-marathon. Could I possibly be an inspiration for someone else? I certainly hoped so. In the meantime, I had a race to run.

I was oddly calm as the starting gun went off. I moved slowly with the crowd, stepping over articles of layered clothing that some runners had already shed. *How inconsiderate! Runners could trip over these!* I crossed the starting line and started the timer on my watch, then switched it over to the heart rate monitor so I could keep an eye on my heart rate during the race. I mentally rehearsed my strategy: *Run for a block or so, then walk before my heart rate gets too high. Continue for 13.1 miles.* I could feel my muscles starting to warm up and relax. I dropped my garbage bag into a sidewalk trash bin at the first half-mile.

Conversation from a group of runners to my right floated over the thumps of running shoes hitting the pavement. "It's our first half-marathon!" three women and a man, all wearing New Orleans Saints jerseys, were saying to another runner as they passed. "Mine too!" I offered. "Well, run with us, then!" they invited. I knew they were faster than I was, so I demurred and said, "Have a great race!"

I was far enough back from the fastest runners that I was in a pack of racers who, like me, were alternating between running and walking. By the first mile, many of us had settled into intervals, and I laughed to myself about having fretted that I would be the only one who wouldn't be running the entire 13.1 mile distance. Ha! So silly, I was.

Outrunning Age

I relaxed and started noticing the people who were running nearby. Where on earth did the runner in front of me, a man who looked to be in his late forties, get those crazy compression socks? A cartoon cat grinned at me from the back of each calf with every step he took. Ahead of him were two women dressed like Minnie Mouse. Their spirit of fun made me smile. Perhaps that was what this was really about—enjoying the experience and not taking myself so seriously. The cats, the Minnies, the Saints, and I all clustered in a pack, unofficial teammates for a while.

My mind settled into the mental routine I had had during training. *Check my heart rate. Check my energy level.* I had trained on an empty stomach to teach my body to draw from fat stores for energy instead of carbs and glucose. I had brought a glucose gel with me just in case but hoped I wouldn't have to use it. I had heard stories of how runners *bonk*—when they use up all the fuel in their bodies—causing them to feel heavy, slow down, and even throw up. I wanted to avoid bonking if I could.

Oh darn, now I have to pee. Crap. I'm not even a mile into the race, and I'm going to have to sacrifice minutes to get in line and pee. I didn't want to be the menopausal lady who ended up with wet pants because I didn't listen to my body, so I pulled over at water station number one, trotted to the Porta Potty stand, got in line, and tried not to think about how much time this stop was adding to my race time. As I finally stepped in and stripped down, the blast of the thirty-three-degree air hit my bare skin. I envied men who could relieve themselves while remaining mostly dressed.

Race Day, Take Two

Back on the road, I tried not to focus on how many miles I had left, and instead concentrated on how lovely the oak trees were as they arched over the boulevard in the old neighborhood we ran through. The Craftsman-style cottages were familiar to me, as I had driven down this boulevard thousands of times. I felt as if old friends lined the streets, silently encouraging me as my shoes hit the pavement.

I began waving to and thanking the police officers who were stationed along the course, who had given up a Sunday morning to handle traffic. I liked that despite the cold, people had come out to cheer us on. It made me appreciate my community.

My body was feeling good. I ran up to my target heart rate and then walked for a while, alternating between walking briskly and sprinting through the LSU campus and past Tiger Stadium. I cruised through miles two, three, four, and five, having run this path many times in training. My hands were warm, and I was grateful for the hand warmers in my gloves, as the wind chill made the already-cold air feel much colder.

A delightful surprise was about to break through. My story was that, being a Louisiana native, I ran better in hot weather. Ninety percent humidity and ninety-degree heat were no problem. I was well aware of how my attitude and internal narrative shaped my day, so I had caught myself that morning while I was dressing for the race. I had been telling myself how miserable I was going to be in the cold. *Whoa! What am I creating for myself?* I thought. *Maybe my body knows better than my*

Outrunning Age

thoughts; maybe it knows that it will perform better in this cold than my mind thinks it can. I need to be open to finding out. I certainly wasn't going to bail on the race, so I held open the possibility that the cold wouldn't bother me.

What a surprise! I was very comfortable as the miles passed. I had guessed correctly for my clothing, as it was right in the Goldilocks zone: not too much, not too little, but just right. I relaxed and just kept going, just like in training: running up to my target heart rate, then walking briskly until it came back down. Repeat.

Mile seven took us through a residential neighborhood near LSU. Broad live oak limbs shaded the yards, and lovely houses filled the streets that were named for colleges. This neighborhood was built in the 1930s and '40s for professors and was one of my favorites.

The runners had thinned out by this time. As I turned the last corner heading back onto the main boulevard, I caught sight of a bright pink hat bobbing up and down about fifty yards ahead of me. *Is that Tiffany?* As I got closer, I saw that it was indeed Tiffany, the woman whom Tom had helped across the chasm in Beast for a Day. I was concerned that she was limping and not running at her usual pace. "I've hurt my knee," she said after we hugged.

"Oh no! How are you doing?" I replied.

"Making it, but you need to go on. This is your first, so don't let me hold you back."

"I'll see you at the finish line," I said, breaking into a run and drawing away.

As I ran, I thought back to all the runners I knew

Race Day, Take Two

who had inspired me. Tiffany, whose social media was filled with photos she took every time she worked out and raced, had certainly been one. I admired that she was reaching for her commitment to do this half-marathon, even though she didn't feel her best. So much of training for anything is persevering and not letting how you feel give you excuses to quit.

My thoughts drifted back to the first race I had ever run. It was shortly after my divorce, and I was still a fairly new runner. I had debated whether or not to do the Reindeer Run in downtown Baton Rouge. It was a 5K, which doesn't seem like much to me now, but at the time I had only run a distance of two consecutive miles. My friend Jim Taylor offered to run the race with me, and I signed up. Jim was a decade older than I, a longtime runner who ran six miles every day on his lunch break. Tall and slender, with a good sense of humor and thoughtful encouragement, he was a good choice as a running partner for my first race. He kindly slowed his pace down to match mine, and we tooled along for 3.1 miles, tracking part of the path that I was now running in my half-marathon. Even though that was the only time Jim and I ever ran together, he remains one of my inspirations. A few years ago, he was diagnosed with primary lateral sclerosis, and he gradually lost his ability to walk.

I reflected on how frustrated I was when I couldn't run because of my knee injury. I had wondered if I would be permanently injured and unable to run ever again. After I healed, I thought of running as a privilege, an ability not to be taken for granted. Every training session since then, I told my body how appreciative I was of its ability. It is easy to take a pass on training when mental and physical conditions aren't perfect, and there were many days when I wanted to skip out on a scheduled training run—but I didn't. I knew Jim would love to still be able to run. *I can run*, I thought, *and today, Jim, I run on your behalf and in your honor.*

Miles eight and nine circled the LSU lakes, and I was again on familiar ground. The usual chattering squirrels weren't out today, and the intermittent sunlight glittered on the water as hundreds of runners pattered by. I appreciated all of the volunteers who stood out in the cold to hand us cups of water and sports drinks. One in particular enthusiastically pointed at the ground by the ten-mile sign and shouted, "That's ten! Only three more to go!" I broke out my glucose gel pack and sucked it down, refreshed for the final three miles.

I checked in with my body. My heart rate was holding steady at 155. My hips were aching a little from the pounding, but it was a pleasant ache. It meant that I was exactly where I wanted to be at this mileage and that I would still have energy left to make a burst of speed toward the finish line.

Up ahead, a photographer was standing in the middle of the road at the top of a small hill, which meant that if I wanted to get a decent race photo, I would need to actually run instead of walk so that both feet would be off the ground at the same time. I confess that I had looked up how to get good race photos; I wanted

Race Day, Take Two

evidence that I had done this race! I made it past the photographer, doing my best but not wasting energy. I smiled as I passed him, enjoying the day.

I was still a half-mile from the finish line. I kept going, enjoying the sight of all the runners ahead of me. I finally rounded the corner to the home stretch. I was once again overcome with emotion as I saw the inflatable finish line two blocks ahead, framing the Louisiana State Capitol building in its rectangle. Bystanders and runners who had finished crowded the sidewalks, cheering us on.

Music mingled with the cheers, and I suddenly heard my name. I looked left and saw three of my BTR Mudder runner friends who were in the pre-race photo we had taken together. They were younger and faster and had finished quite a while before, and now here they were, clapping and woo-hooing for *me*! I teared up as I realized that they had waited for me in the bitter cold, and that kind act caught me by surprise. They all knew this was my first half-marathon, and I was very moved by their support. It was a beautiful way to be escorted across the finish line.

I barely heard my name called over the loudspeaker as I crossed. I was now that sixty-year-old woman who had completed her first half-marathon, and I couldn't have been prouder of myself. I had stuck with my training to complete my goal, and had run 159 miles during that time. I had earned the 13.1 half-marathon sticker.

Chapter 11
What's Next?

> *When you get to a place where you understand that love and belonging, your worthiness, is a birthright and not something you have to earn, anything is possible.*
> —BRENÉ BROWN

I should have known it was coming. "So, when are you doing a full marathon?" Ugh. I was still enjoying the badass feeling from completing my first half-marathon and fulfilling my commitment to myself, and these well-intentioned questions immediately propelled me into thinking that no matter what I did, it would never be quite good enough. Those questions also touched the tender spot of my own question about what I wanted to do next.

I was initially bummed out when I saw my race stats. I had finished 1,937 out of 2,192 runners, with a time of three hours and six minutes—which would have been under three hours had I not had to wait in line for a potty break—twice. Oh, thank you, menopause. I did see the humor in it, however, and returned my focus to the fact that I had completed the race. Even so, to be honest, I did wish I had been a teeny bit faster.

Then it hit me: Brandon's race pace was almost twice as fast as mine; that meant he could run a marathon in just a little longer than it took me to run a half-marathon. I got a sudden jolt of pride. I may not have the speed, but I had the conditioning. I could do three hours of continuous exercise and feel good afterward. Yes, my hips were sore, and I would definitely take it easy for the next couple of days, but I could hang in there, something I couldn't have done five years before. *I'm a badass!*

After the half-marathon, I dialed back my training and relaxed. It felt good to be off a rigorous training schedule and yet still miss the discipline of it. A few weeks after the race, I danced with thirty-nine other costumed women for three miles in our neighborhood nighttime Mardi Gras parade. (Whenever anyone asked about my recent runs, I would say, "I did the Southdowns Mardi Gras Parade 5K.") Following that, I ran the Mardi Gras Mambo 10K, enjoying the company of fellow BTR Mudders and my ability to comfortably run a 10K.

Getting older is sometimes accompanied by the notion that it takes something away that is impossible to get back. If we believe that, we won't try, and this, in my opinion, is one of the reasons that the world gets smaller for older people as the years go by. I was delighted to be presented with evidence against this

What's Next?

paradigm when I compared my first Mardi Gras Mambo time to my finish time of that race two years later—I was six minutes faster! I took the time to appreciate my ability to stick with my goal and do the work it took to get there. It was also rewarding to see the improvement in my body.

But the question of what to do next was still there, and I wasn't sure of the answer. As the summer progressed, I felt two competing urges.

"When are you doing your next half?" I heard more than once. "You've inspired me to train for one. Want to do it with me?" I didn't know if I was obliged to run another half now that I was inspiring others or if I would let them down if I didn't.

From the moment I crossed the finish line, I was clear that I was not interested in committing to training to run a full marathon—but another half? I looked at my options. One upcoming half-marathon was going to start within a mile of my house, and I wondered if I should do that one. Another race was coming up on the Mississippi Gulf Coast, and many of my runner friends liked it because the run is along the beach. That one could be fun. Round and round my thoughts went, switching between convincing myself to commit to another race and allowing myself to say no. Should or shouldn't. Should or shouldn't. If there had been another half-marathon the week after my first one, I might have done it, but waiting until another fall race cycle didn't motivate me.

I had checked in with my body after the race and

could feel the toll it had taken on me. I was okay, but I needed several days to recover. A full marathon distance of 26.2 miles was twice as long as a half-marathon, so I could easily be moving for six to seven hours, twice the time of my half. I didn't know if I wanted to put my body under that stress. I did know that I would need a lot of mental energy for the training time, quite possibly an entire year. I knew that it would be within my grasp if I decided to do it, but I didn't know if that was how I wanted to focus my creative energy. I drove myself crazy for several weeks with these questions.

I played classical piano from first grade all the way through my freshman year in college, and I was pretty good at it. I had an ear for music and a sense of musicality that infused soul into my playing. Practice time became an escape, a meditation, and a way for me to give rein to my perfectionism. In high school, I reluctantly played in the local piano competitions my teacher had started. I usually placed in the top five but never grabbed first place.

I was good enough, however, that as I approached college age, the adults in my world asked if I planned to major in music. I wasn't drawn to it but took a semester of piano instruction my freshman year anyway. I wanted to please my teacher—he was my then boyfriend's father—so I worked hard, practicing scales and piano exercises for hours. The LSU music building had a hallway full of rooms just large enough to hold an upright piano, and the cacophony of notes wafted out most hours of the day and night.

What's Next?

Late one afternoon, I had just finished my practice session for the day and was leaving the hall when I heard warmup arpeggios followed by a beautiful piano performance. I paused for a moment, filled with both awe and envy at the rapid dexterity and the interpretation that was producing the sounds. I peeked through the glass door of the room and saw Willis Delony, whom I had occasionally competed against in my high school piano competitions. He was why I never got first place.

I had eventually told my high school teacher that I would no longer play in any competition that Willis entered. He was just *that* good (and in fact went on to become a professional concert pianist). I was talented, but he was gifted. I knew then and there that I was not willing to put in the hours and energy it would take to *maybe* put me close to Willis's league; I just didn't have the interest. I was happy with what I had achieved. The last big song I learned to play to performance standard was Debussy's "Clair De Lune." I soon moved on to other creative callings.

When I thought back to that moment in college, I knew I had made my decision about running. I was not going to train back up for another half-marathon for now. The energy and dedication it would take was more than I was willing to spend. I had proven to myself that I could do it, and I was proud that I had set a goal and reached it. I gave myself permission to change my mind at any time in the future, but for now, I was clear.

What is bigger for me now is finding a baseline of health and fitness that can sustain me through my sixties and into my seventies, eighties, and beyond. I asked myself what I wanted for my health and fitness and what actions I was willing to commit to in order to get it. This led to clarity about my long-term goals.

What excites me now is staying at a fitness level where I can run a 10K any time I want without having to up my training. I have added yoga and strength training to keep fit, flexible, strong, and balanced. These are doable, with a couple of short runs added in during the week and one long run on weekends. I know that I will have to adapt as the years go by, but for now, this feels right. What a relief to have made this decision!

One Year Later

The seven-and-a-half mile point for the Louisiana Marathon and Half-Marathon course is a half mile from my house. This year, the unseasonably warm January weather had caused the Japanese magnolias and redbud trees to jump the starting gun, and the pink of their blooms made a shock of contrast with the turquoise blue of the sky. I thought of how beautiful it was going to be for the day's runners and how, one year before, I was on that course, appreciating the neighbors who had come out to cheer on the runners. I was at peace with my choice to not participate this year.

As I thought of my friends who were going to run the year's races, I reflected back on the experiences that training for my first half-marathon had brought me. The feeling of being an imposter runner was gone.

What's Next?

I knew that I didn't need the half-marathon completion medal to be a "real" runner, but I was proud of not only doing the race but also facing my self-doubts about what I was capable of "at this age." By doing shorter races throughout my training, I had surprised myself by twice coming in first in my age group in a 5K. I *was* capable of more than I had thought.

I learned, too, of the various personalities different running groups have, and where I fit in. I hadn't meshed well with one road running group I had tried. I had felt like an outsider in a group where pace, form, and running accomplishments were the currency for belonging. When I try to fit in where I don't belong, I suffer and feel bad about myself. I felt much more at home in the trail and ultra running communities, where people celebrated the fact that others were just out there participating.

I was particularly charmed by two moments in the trail running community. The first came two minutes after I had signed up for my first trail race after Beast for a Day. The race, called Run for the Hills, covered over five miles of trails in one of Louisiana's state parks. It was sponsored by Q50 Races and organized by race director Cesar Torres. Shortly after registering, I answered the phone and a deep, exuberant, Latin-flavored voice exclaimed, "Meh-LEEN-dah! I'm so happy to meet you!" Cesar continues to win my heart, as he dedicates portions of each registration to charity, and he has banned paper and plastic cups from the race course in service to sustainable practices. I learned from Cesar to bring bug spray, as running tights, wooded trails, and chiggers are an unhappy mix.

The second moment came during Walker Higgins's fall race, the Cane Field Classic, a seven-mile combo of a one-mile, a four-mile, and a two-mile run down various pathways through a Louisiana sugar cane field. I was run-walking the four-mile section and just finishing up mile three when I noticed a man I knew from the BTR Mudders, running and walking alongside another man from the BTR Mudders, a man who was new to running. The first man was a blazing fast runner, so I was surprised to see him tracking his friend's run-walk pace. I quickly realized that he was there to coach and support a new runner. I smiled, touched by his generous gesture.

We have all needed someone to encourage us at times, to gently and nonjudgmentally help us locate our confidence when we have temporarily lost it. I was so grateful for all of the people who scooped me up when I was discouraged about my physical ability, who hung in there with me until I reached the finish line—and beyond. Life is like that sometimes. When we think we can't do something, we get so lost in trying to avoid discomfort that we tell ourselves we "couldn't possibly," and then we never try. A supportive community helps us reframe that thinking. I know I couldn't do half of what I have done in my life without friends who were willing to pace with me.

What's Next?

Questioning Myself

I had some flash when I was younger. I was on commercials that ran all over Louisiana and recognized everywhere I went. I have been in made-for-TV movies and worked in the film industry. My voice has been heard on commercials nationwide and in other countries, and I have won awards for my work—yet I always felt that I needed to do more.

No matter what I had done, it wasn't ever enough. Stand out *even more* from the crowd. Write a book—write a *best-selling* book. Promote myself on TV—promote myself on *national* TV. Run a half-marathon—run a *marathon*. Run an *ultramarathon*. Maximize my potential.

This feeling was driven by an inner directive that said, *Whatever you do, don't be ordinary*—as if being ordinary were akin to the death of my soul. There was always someone who was more accomplished than I, and I would compare myself to them in my unconscious mission to not be ordinary, thinking, *I need to do that, too*. It never stopped. All those expectations weighed me down. Perhaps at age sixty, it was time to take a mature look at what was driving this competition in me.

Over the course of the months of my half-marathon training, I gradually shifted my story. I started by asking myself what would happen if I released this inner narrative I had run all my life. I wondered if it were possible to overcome the momentum of all those repeated thoughts through the years, to have it just be *okay* that I didn't push myself to be the Awesomest At Everything. I asked myself if I could write for the enjoyment of it without having to make the result into a book. What if being ordinary was something I had been all along? What if it would give my life more meaning and purpose than I realized? Perhaps I had been discounting something worth valuing, focusing instead on achievements—but those things are important, too. Was there such a thing as Awesomely Ordinary? It was something to ponder, and I felt it was important to do so.

I think we humans suffer from the plague of low self-worth. I know this has gripped me by the throat at times. We are born lovely little creatures who naturally think we are awesome, but through the *drip-drip-drip* of criticism and negative opinions from others, the world slowly brainwashes us into believing that we are not. We evolve coping mechanisms of performance designed to avoid criticism and to validate us. While that tactic feels good in the moment, it has an expiration date, because it doesn't address the real purpose of accepting ourselves. I think of what my friend and coach Charlie Bloom says: "We can't get enough of what we don't really want."

But wait. What if I accept—deeply accept—that I am a terrific person who has flaws and graces, moments of perfection and imperfection? I could set aside my list of unspoken expectations: return to a smaller size, write that book, produce that movie, do better at keeping in touch with friends, eat four servings of veggies at every meal, and take my supplements every single day. I could tie my sense of love for myself to being-ness instead of accomplishment-ness, to lose the habit of self-criticism and instead listen to a voice of self-love. I could truly own that I have worth and value no matter what I do or don't do. I could quit apologizing for not being able to do what I used to be able to do. I may have lost some speed, but I could focus instead on the endurance I've gained, and the self-respect that comes from being someone who gets out there and tries.

Now that would be some Good Work.

At This Age

One of the outcomes of my hours spent training involved long reflection on what it means to me to be this age. I turned sixty-one a month after my half-marathon. As I write this, I am a month away from turning sixty-two. Facing my beliefs about aging involved finding a balance between learning to accept what won't change no matter how much I train or apply moisturizer and reminding myself that my capacity is often greater than what I believe it is.

I have come to love the question, "What if I can do more now than I could when I was younger?" *More* is not limited to physical ability; it also applies to our ability to work through fears and limiting beliefs in a way that was not available to us in our younger years. It is about having courage to try something new, and knowing that failure isn't terminal, it's just feedback. Challenging our self-imposed limitations fuels excitement about life.

Aging also brings a greater acquaintance with loss; accumulating years and increasingly frequent losses are partners. I think of how love involves the risk that one day, a person we love will no longer be there. The courageous choice is to love anyway, instead of building a shield around the heart. This means that sometimes we collide with the discomfort of sadness.

I was fortunate; I didn't lose anyone really close to me until I was in my fifties. When the losses started, however, they came in a tsunami. First one friend was diagnosed with cancer, then another, and then another with a terminal neurological illness. They passed away one after the other. Then my runner friend Andy died of injuries sustained after being hit by a car. The topper was my dad, who died at age ninety-one, three days after Tom and I married. It was a lot to take in, but the wise part of me collected support and made a conscious effort to focus on the things I was grateful for, the beautiful things in my life, instead of ruminating over what I had lost. I thought of the Serenity Prayer and tried to "accept the things I cannot change." Some days it was hard. Sometimes I am wistful for earlier times in my life when loss didn't hit me with such an impact.

How do we learn to accept that loss is simply a part of life and that embracing it doesn't have to mean that we lose our enthusiasm for life? How do we recognize that there are many as-yet-to-be-discovered opportunities ahead? I look at my mother-in-law, a zesty ninety-eight years old, who has outlived her peers but not her health. She thrives on time spent with her children, grandchildren, and great-grandchildren. Her face lights up with delight and she squeals with excitement

What's Next?

whenever she talks with family. I notice carefully, and I wonder whether I hold myself back from showing how much I enjoy someone. Perhaps retaining delight in the little moments of life balances out the moments of loss. Conflicting emotions, such as sadness and joy, often live side by side.

Loss isn't just about losing people dear to us, it is also about losing bits and pieces of our younger selves. Loss creeps up on us through the years, sneaking things away bit by bit, prompting justifications of *okay, just this once* or *it's not a big deal*. This is followed by a gradual awareness that the sleeveless shirt you wore last year looks different and that maybe you should look for a shirt that covers arms that can no longer be described as "guns"—or just wear the damn shirt anyway. New decisions about old patterns.

Loss can show up abruptly, an uninvited guest that wallops us upside the head with the news that Things Will Never Be the Same Again. My childhood report cards and school photos washed away in the space of minutes in the flood, leaving me with memories but little evidence of past experiences that matter to me.

Getting up off the floor now involves sound effects I didn't make when I was younger. No matter how much I train, I am still slower than I was in my forties. Even brilliantly talented marathon record-setter Meb Keflezighi slowed down as he aged, so why would I expect to be different? I knew this conceptually, but my body's changes that come with age still catch me by surprise. I don't like that I occasionally find myself

Outrunning Age

grieving for What Used To Be: my smooth skin, my younger body shape.

I work at letting go of what I can't change because I know that there isn't enough grief in the world to turn back the clock. I would rather live in gratitude for all the wonderful people, experiences, and capacity that I still have instead of living in a cloud of sadness. When I catch myself visiting my sadness, I actively look for something to be grateful for—and something is always there. Soon, my sadness eases. The wisdom of age allows me to shift this in a way that I couldn't when I was younger.

I am discovering a regular tenderness toward myself. I am accepting that the unhelpful negative voice in my head will likely never shut up, but it now shares space with a quiet, kind voice that acknowledges me for just being me. I live more in gratitude now than I used to, having learned to better observe myself when I focus on what is missing instead of what is present. Having compassion for myself has expanded to having more compassion for others. I know I am capable of projecting self-judgment onto someone else as a way of avoiding dealing with it, although that has gotten less frequent. Through miles of training and becoming more effective at managing my thoughts, I have learned that it just feels better to be kind and grateful than self-critical. I have become my own cheerleader for my inner kindergartener. *Yay, Melinda!*

I also now see that I have more compassion for myself, for being someone who tries, who is willing to hurl herself off of a high platform to see what flying

What's Next?

is like, who runs slower than she would like but runs anyway. Perhaps it's not about outrunning age, since we can't. What is important is not the participation medals, the bibs, the pace. Maybe it's about of running *with* age and meeting life with grace and a sense of adventure. The words *I am* have power to shape my future. *I am* a runner. *I am* a woman who grows more self-aware, empowered, and wise as I accumulate years.

Now that I have a half-marathon behind me, I look forward to cheering for friends and strangers who are running today, to pay it forward for those who did it for me. There will come a time when I have run for the last time, but today is not that day.

Acknowledgments

When I first started training for a half-marathon, I wasn't sure I would be able to do it. This book is the same way. I have written professionally for years in my career, but prior to this point, I had never been able to cross the finish line with a manuscript—until now. I may have done the writing, but I was encouraged and inspired by so many people.

My running inspirations were many and reached across time. Andy Hauck, you showed me what the daily life of a lifelong runner looks like. Thanks for connecting me with Lorraine Moller, whose love of and accomplishments in running continue to inspire me.

My BTR Mudder friends: Walker Higgins, Gabby Higgins, Vanessa Le, Mike Harris, Jason Cheek, Kenniann Henley, Jamie Higgins, Kristin Nowlin, and Mischa Pizzolato, along with the rest of you, you all inspired me. Thank you for not only welcoming me into your community but also for supporting our family during the flood of 2016.

Outrunning Age

Gwen Zywicke, we have shared many miles and conversations together as this book is being brought forth. Thank you for being my running partner, my encouragement, my inspiration, and my friend. You make such a difference in my life.

Jennifer Doucet, Matthew and Taylor Naylor: so much fun to run together as a family. Well, not exactly together, as I just get to watch your backs as we run, but starting together and reconnecting after makes running that much richer. Sadly, my amazing mom, "B" Eddards, did not get to see this book published. She was a lifetime cheerleader and inspiration to me.

My Ontological Coaching community. Y'all heard all my doubts and struggles with my commitment. Speaking it in front of you helped bring it into reality. Your believing in me helped me to believe in myself and cut myself some slack. Sometimes we just need that.

I had a big cheering and coaching section for my writing process, starting with my mastermind ladies: Terri Britt, Carol Gunn, and Lana Kontos. How many conversations did we have about our respective writings and programs? Thank you for supporting me as I brought this manuscript to completion. I value our Tuesday conversations.

Sandi Way and Bert Fife, you both were so supportive and encouraging of my writing and suffered through many creative explorations with me in the past. I can feel you both still rooting for me from the "Other Side" as you used to say, Bert.

Jan Bernard, thank you for sharing writing sessions

Acknowledgments

with me as we both worked on our respective books. Authors Christopher McDougall and Jen Miller: your writings about the experience of running helped me see what is possible. Nick Ortego, your expertise about the human body played a big part in allowing me to embrace the idea that I could do the race.

Shruti Chowdhary, the gifts of your time, talent, encouragement and wisdom are a big part of why this book is being published. Thank you for making the commitment to zooming and holding me accountable, along with helping me get out of my stuck spots.

A special thank you to Brandon Eddards, whom I have had the pleasure of seeing grow into an amazing person. I wouldn't have had the courage to start training for a race without your pushing me. By listening to my struggles as I trained, you repaid me for all the conversations we had through the years when I listened to you. I'm so glad we are family.

First readers, I appreciate y'all so much. Your kind and thoughtful feedback gave me the encouragement I needed to keep going.

Over many hours across several years, Martha Bullen and I deepened our friendship and brought forth this book. Martha, you know I couldn't have done this without you. You are an inspiring, insightful, and expert book coach, and I have learned so much from you. I am honored to be your friend.

Tom Naylor, whenever I need you, you are there for me. I can't imagine my life without you. I'm glad we are doing the marathon of life together.

So You Want to Start Exercising

I was at the gym last winter, during a rare below-freezing day in Baton Rouge, experimenting with running on a treadmill. I had wiped out spectacularly a few years back, and had avoided treadmills ever since. Running on my usual route that day wasn't an option, since there was ice everywhere, so I decided to face my trepidation and get back on the mechanical horse, so to speak. There were several of us all in a row, facing an aisle, and I was lured into a reverie by the whirring sound of the machine and the repetitive thumping of our shoes.

As I glanced up, I saw an older gentleman passing by on the aisle, followed by what looked like an aide. He walked with difficulty, swinging his hip to move his leg forward instead of simply walking in a line. He paused, looked up at all of us on the treadmill, and said, "Showoffs!" His smile said there was a lot of pain behind that word, and that it revealed more about him than those of us on the treadmills.

I was so surprised that I said nothing. Later, I wished I had said, "That's not the right phrase. The right phrase is, 'Way to go!'"

If you're ready to start exercising, my message for you is "Way to go!" Here are some things to keep in mind as you begin training.

1. Start at your own pace. It can be tempting to just jump in and overdo it, and this tendency is something that even seasoned exercisers can get caught up in. Overdoing it is where injuries can happen, which may sour someone on the idea of exercising at all. Your body knows what it can do, so make sure to listen to it.

2. Make it simple. I started running because all I had to do was to put on running shoes, and that minimized my opportunity for excuses as to why I didn't need to exercise. When I started, the idea of finding a gym, coming up with a weightlifting plan, or joining a class felt overwhelming, so running or walking were the simplest kinds of exercise I thought I could continue. In addition, there are plenty of online videos that you can follow along with without leaving your house. Just make sure you find one that is geared to your current fitness level.

3. Explore. Over the years, I've done walking, running, weight training, Pilates, Yoga, Yogalates and a multitude of different exercise classes. Some I liked and stuck with, some I didn't. Give yourself permission to not

So You Want to Start Exercising

like something—but give it an honest shot first. One approach that works is to set a time frame to try a new exercise, and then keep that commitment. Once the time frame is up, evaluate if it's something you'd like to continue. Different personalities have different preferences. You may like the energy and accountability of a group class. Or you may find you enjoy the solitude of training on your own. Finding your own groove is what exploration is about!

4. Aim for 1% improvement. I don't know about you, but my ego will often offer up completely unrealistic notions about how fast I should be progressing—particularly after only a short time. I've learned to manage my expectations by focusing on my *process* instead of my progress. By that I've learned to give myself kudos for maintaining a consistent training program, instead of constantly evaluating myself for what I can do and how/if I'm improving. What surprised me was that focusing on the process brought about results as a lovely byproduct. An incremental 1% improvement over time adds up nicely.

5. Appreciate and acknowledge. There are days when I put on my running clothes, and only walk slowly around the block. And others where I'm ready to go for miles. You won't always be in the mood for exercise or feel like doing it and that's okay. Give yourself credit for ANY exercise you do, and acknowledge yourself for overcoming any resistance you may have for doing it. This helps you create the important habit of talking kindly to yourself, which in the long run, leads to a bigger feeling of self-worth and confidence. And I don't know about you, but I'm always on board for more of that!

Outrunning Age
Questions for Reflection

1. Could you relate to Melinda's struggle with aging? In what ways?

2. Of all the stories in the book, which one has stayed with you the most and why?

3. What beliefs do you have about getting older?

4. Are you worried that you might miss out on things you used to be able to do?

5. What is one thing you love about your body?

6. What is one thing you appreciate about your body?

7. What inspired you most about Melinda's story?

8. What would you like to try or do differently after reading this book?

9. If you could ask the author anything, what would it be?

About the Author

Melinda Walsh is a relentlessly creative award-winning communicator whose experience both in front of and behind the camera has made her an expert in the intentional use of story to make transformational shifts.

Drawing from her experience as a professional marketer, mentor and certified ontological coach, Melinda is on a mission to help women rewrite their story and step fully into their own power.

She lives in Baton Rouge with her husband Tom and you can regularly find her running the LSU lakes.

To learn more or contact Melinda,
visit www.melindawalsh.com.

Made in the USA
Columbia, SC
12 February 2023